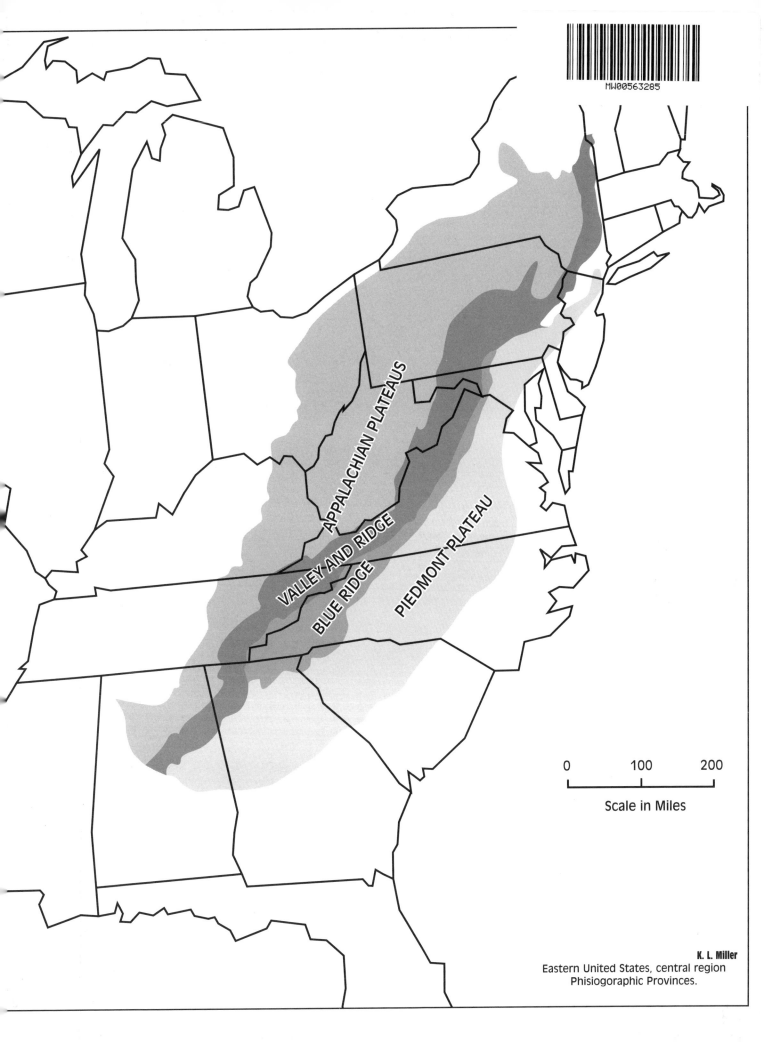

APPALACHIAN PLATEAUS

VALLEY AND RIDGE

BLUE RIDGE

PIEDMONT PLATEAU

MW00563285

0   100   200

Scale in Miles

K. L. Miller
Eastern United States, central region
Phisiogoraphic Provinces.

Appalachian
Conquest

C&O, N&W, Virginian and Clinchfield Cross the Mountains

by
Eugene L. Huddleston, Ph.D.

Published 2002 by
TLC Publishing Inc.
1387 Winding Creek Lane • Lynchburg, Virginia 24503-3776
and
The Chesapeake & Ohio Historical Society, Inc.
P.O. Box 79 • Clifton Forge, Virginia 24422

Appalachian
Conquest

C&O, N&W, Virginian and Clinchfield Cross the Mountains

ISBN 1-883089-79-4
Library of Congress Catalog Card Number: 2002104983

Cover Illustrations:

Background: The spectacular fall scenery of western Virginia's George Washington National Forest as seen from Moss Run on the C&O's right of way. Photo from 1979 by Kenneth L. Miller.

Each of the three Pocahontas Roads is represented on the front cover and the Clinchfield on the back.
Front Cover: From top left: Virginian: E.L. Huddleston, N&W: B.D. Martin, C&O: Wayne Sherwin,
Back Cover: Clinchfield: Everett N. Young, N&W: E.L. Huddleston

Layout and Design by Kenneth L. Miller • Miller Design & Photography • Salem, Va. 24153

Table of Contents

Preface

Revising and expanding *Appalachian Crossing: The Pocahontas Roads* attempts freezing in time some scenes of of railroading in southern Appalachia when man, machine, and nature seemed in balance. Now the balance has tipped in favor of man and machine "conquering" nature. In flatter areas of United States east of the Mississippi, "progress" does not usually despoil the landscape. The land simply fills up. But in the hills, mountains, and valleys of Appalachia, progress usually means four-lane highways that are not just laid down on the land. It means earth moving machines that scrape down summits and fill up valleys to the extent that tunnels are seldom deemed necessary, since dynamite and scrapers can level just about any mountain. The same goes for getting to a mineable seam of coal. No reason to go underground when dynamite, dragline, and shovel can level the tops of the "green-muffled" hills and expose two or three feet of good steam or metallurical bituminous. The alteration of the old forms of nature are accompanied by a decreasing railroad mileage in Appalachia. The shining rails are too often gone, and the right of ways returning either to a natural state or being converted to public nature trails. Even where rails remain, they become hard to differentiate from a profusion of foliage.

To keep within the confines of an average sized book, one must limit coverage of the railroads crossing the Appalachian chain, and one should keep to the roads he knows best. That is why the first edition concentrated on the so called Pocahontas roads. Geographically, "Pocahontas" applies to several contiguous seams of coal which slope downward, westerly, mostly in McDowell and Wyoming counties in West Virginia, until they drop below drainage perhaps thirty miles from their eastern most exposure along the flank of Great Flattop Mountain. The thickest of these seams, Pocahontas No. 3, became—through the tonnage mined—the second most important seam in the history of West Virginia mining. The seam was typically twelve feet thick, and the Norfolk and Western and Virginian Railways were the chief beneficiaries of hauling this coal to market, although Chesapeake and Ohio shared with the Virginian service to some mines in the Pocahontas field. Historically, the term applies to a particular region established by the United States Railroad Administration during the takeover of the nation's railroads by the federal government during World War I. It was only after some administrative problems that the chief coal hauling roads in the southern Appalachian coal fields were taken from the larger Eastern region and given their own federal manager and identification. Included in this new and relatively small region were the Norfolk and Western, the Virginian, and the Chesapeake and Ohio (excluding the latter's line from Cincinnati to Chicago).

The Pocahontas seams were not the only important sources of top quality sub-bituminous in the World War I era. All three roads served mines tapping seams identified as "smokeless." The United States navy required low-volatile or smokeless coal for its ships. That gave to the three roads a unity of purpose. One problem in the transportation of Pocahontas and other low-volatile coal to Tidewater ports was the failure of the President of the Virginian to cooperate with its then keen rival, the Norfolk and Western, for a common route across the Blue Ridge barrier to Tidewater. The new regional manager, being a former N&W President, made sure the two cooperated. After the railroads were returned to private ownership in 1920, the ICC kept the Pocahontas designation for the three coal roads in its accounting summaries.

These were the three roads, then, of the original printing of *Appalachian Crossing, the Pocahontas Roads.* By historical development, topography, and geography, the Clinchfield Railroad (or as known during World War I, the Carolina, Clinchfield, and Ohio) deserves inclusion as a Pocahontas road. However, during the War it was assigned to the Southern Region; the CC&O apparently lacked enough status as a carrier of low-volatile, or smokeless, coal to be included. Certainly it lacked facilities along the coast line of South Carolina (its logical outlet to the sea) for transferring coal at a safe harbor into ocean going colliers. And Virginian, C&O, and N&W had such facilities.

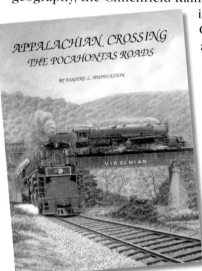

Thankfully, World Wars I and II are both long gone, but the passage of time has affected the identities of the railroads in question. By the mid-1980s, Chesapeake & Ohio was no longer a viable marking on locomotives and cars, its new name being a trendy initialism—CSX Transportation. The Virginian Railway had been the first to lose its identity, for late in 1959 it was absorbed by the Norfolk and Western, which itself, at about the same time C&O became CSX, decided its corporate future lay in combination with the Southern, whose slogan "The Southern Serves the South" almost everyone over 50 recalls! How the Clinchfield ended up under the CSX umbrella is a little tricky. Let George Drury, in his *Historical Guide to North American Railroads* (Kalmbach, 1985) tell part of what happened: "In 1924 the Atlantic Coast Line and Louisville and Nashville railroads jointly leased the properties of the Carolina, Clinchfield, and Ohio. The two lessees named the Clinchfield Railroad Company...as the operating organization." In 1967 the Seaboard and Atlantic Coast Line merged to form the Seaboard Coast Line, and in 1983 the Family Lines merger effectively did away with the Clinchfield as an entity separate from the L&N and SCL, major components of the Family Lines. Finally, with the whole line intact, the Clinchfield identity was swallowed up by CSX in 1986.

"Appalachian" in this book is broken down into the physiographic provinces comprising the Appalachian chain roughly south of the New York-Pennsylvania border. All four roads cross the same series of four contiguous provinces. From west to east they are the Appalachian Plateau, the Ridge and Valley province, the Great Valley, and the Blue Ridge. These mountain provinces are bordered by the Central Lowlands on the west and the Piedmont region on the east. While the geographical scope of the book can be clearly delineated, the chronological coverage cannot be as clearly fixed or as logically approached. Illustrations in the book date generally from the mid-1940s to the 1990s, with the decade of the of the 1950s and 1960s predominating. Gradually, in the 1950s steam gave way to diesels as motive

power; dieselization was generally completed in 1956 for C&O, 1959 for N&W, 1955 for Virginian, and 1954 for Clinchfield.

The overall aim of the book, then, is to freeze in time the Pocahontas roads amid the Appalachian landscapes. The Introduction justifies from a modern viewpoint inclusion of the Clinchfield as a "Pocahontas road" and reviews the founding and development of the roads and their common need to "conquer" the Appalachian topography. The next chapter reviews, largely with photos, the passage of each road through the physiographic provinces they share in common. And since most of the "romance" of American railroads is associated with passenger trains, a chapter deals with how mountains affected passenger service and passenger locomotive performance. Also, since switchers are often a neglected part of "classic" railroading, another chapter briefly covers the work of switching locomotives in mountain yards, as well as the function of "mine shifters," which in a sense are switchers. A chapter on satellite roads samples some of the short lines attached to the four Pocahontas roads, which were usually dependent on the "parent" road but which could exert a proud independence. And no book on mountain railroads could get by without examining the big engines of the four roads needed to haul freight (mostly soft coal) over the hills and into the valleys and out again to more level topography. A final color section focuses on the scenic splendors of the New River, the majesties of the Blue Ridge barrier, and the engineering needed to gain the summit of the Alleghenies.

Thanks go not only to the people credited with the photos in this book but to those whose expertise has helped shape its content. Chief among those are Thomas W. Dixon, Jr., Bob Harvey, Herb Harwood, Gary Huddleston, James Johnson, Wally Johnson, Ken Marsh, Ken Miller, Kurt Reisweber, Terry Seaks, and Everett Young.

C. K. Marsh
In April 1965 Clinchfield's Elkhorn Turn northbound enters Sandy Ridge Tunnel under the Cumberland Front. With gaps scarce in this mountain wall, construction north from Dante, Virginia, was delayed several years.

"My desire to accomplish something in this world, and particularly to develop the mineral resources of Virginia, and to build up the N&W into a great system has led me into responsibilities which keep my nose right down to the grind-stone, and so far as I can see I do not believe I will be able to get away even for a day."
—Frederick Kimball (President N&W), letter to Charles Hacker, July 22, 1889

Coal traffic unifies the Pocahontas roads. As Ronald D. Eller says, "the fifty million acres or so of coal lands in the Appalachian South was the nation's largest supply of bituminous coal," and so after the 1898 "war with Spain began to generate an increased demand for coal, ...the Appalachian fields entered a period of unparalleled growth." Without access to seams of high quality bituminous thick enough for underground mining, the Virginian Railway would not have come about, and Clinchfield would have struggled to be more than a streak of rust. Even wealthy Norfolk and Western would have been little more than a southeastern regional carrier without that twelve foot thick seam of low-volatile bituminous—Pocahontas No. 3—so valuable that coal operators cooperated in linking access corridors through the seam into an 18-mile tunnel (from Pocahontas, Va., to Dry Creek, W.Va.) to control flooding. N&W altered its expansion plans in 1883 in order to construct a new line to this seam and eventually built westward after tunneling through it! Of the four roads only the Chesapeake and Ohio was built out of Virginia and across the Appalachians with development of coal mining far down in its priorities. It was lucky, though, for C&O that its engineers followed the route sanctioned by George Washington out of his native Virginia to the Ohio; that is, the James River and Kanawha Turnpike and Overland Trail, for that meant the main line would go through the center of the then untapped and practically unknown New River and Kanawha fields, which in time would make the Sewell seam in the New River field the fourth most important seam in the history of West Virginia mining.

But Collis P. Huntington never thought of that. Huntington—flush with success of his Central Pacific linking with the Union Pacific to open the great West—was approached by Virginia backers after the Civil War to finance completion of their road from near the Virginia border to the banks of the Ohio. Here was Huntington's opportunity to achieve even more greatness as an empire builder—linking the Chesapeake and Ohio with what would become the

Sunset route of the Southern Pacific, a line he was pushing toward New Orleans to achieve a true transcontinental. As much as Huntington worked at economic development on the new road—e.g. hiring a city planner to lay out the new city of Huntington, founding a shipbuilding company at the road's terminus on Chesapeake Bay, backing his brother-in-law in founding a car building company in Huntington—he seemed indifferent to building spurs or branches to coal mines. Part of this reticence might have been the ineptness of the geological engineer he hired to report on the natural resources of the new road upon its completion, and part might have been that Huntington was kept busy working out problems of land acquisition and construction beyond the C&O in order to achieve his transcontinental. Even though Huntington's office was in New York, he was a "hands on" administrator, as his collected business papers show, constantly busy planning construction in detail.

But Huntington was not an engineer. Frederick Kimball of the newly formed N&W was. He knew the practical value of coal to industry both in America and England, and he knew how to "prospect" for it. After seeing for himself the thick seam exposed on the east slope of Flattop Mountain near the Virginia-West Virginia border, he directed construction of what would become the main line of the N&W toward the rugged highlands. Henry Huttleston Rogers was, like Huntington, from New England and pretty much self-educated. Having amassed a fortune with Standard Oil, he had the luck to command the loyalty of William N. Page, mining and consulting engineer, who knew the topography of West Virginia, like "a farmer knows a field" in the words of Governor William McCorkle. Rogers and his New York investors learned from Page where the best reserves were; thus Rogers started construction of his line in the middle of an untapped portion of the New River and Pocahontas fields, snubbing both C&O and N&W when the bigger roads (around 1904) refused to share rates at points of connection with his coal field short line. Problem was that starting

Machine in the Garden

Railroads fit in so well with the beauty of the Appalachian landscapes that one is not surprised to discover that artists who are not rail fans have put trains or locomotives into their landscape paintings. In his book *The Machine in the Garden*, Leo Marx explained how in nineteenth century America the train became a metaphor for progress and natural scenery a metaphor for primitivism, two conflicting forces in American intellectual history. That artists in the nineteenth century could introduce puffing trains into peaceful landscapes indicated to Marx that for a time American culture was happily balanced between a need to preserve the past and to move into the future. Trains, which seemed almost alive, could represent the positive side of industrial technology. Thus was achieved a mean between freedom and democracy, (which were wilderness values) and civilization, associated with order, class structure, and industrial manufacturing. In both George Inness' *The Lackawanna Valley* (1855) and Jasper Cropsey's *Starucca Viaduct* (1865), the panoramic landscapes are "home" for the steam powered train coursing through it, and each painter captured the harmony and sublimity of the natural scene. With ever increasing industrialization in the twentieth century no longer were such balanced landscapes possible, most critics argued. Yet many a railroad enthusiast would argue that the possibility of harmonizing trains with nature did not die in the nineteenth century, for such harmony will be achievable as long as there are mountains and steel rails running through them.

construction in the middle of West Virginia, he could only head east with a line that pretty much paralleled the N&W through Virginia. Despite buying property for a terminal on Lake Erie near Toledo, Rogers could find no way to build west out of his part of the great southern West Virginia field—specifically, the upper Guyandotte basin. (N&W and C&O had both started in Tidewater Virginia and moved west through West Virginia.) *Chesapeake & Ohio, Coal and Color* (C&OHS) tells of the frustrations of the Virginian's attempt (even after Rogers' death) to build down the either Guyandotte or Big Coal Rivers toward a Midwest connection.

George Lafayette Carter, founder of the Carolina, Clinchfield, and Ohio (the Clinchfield Railroad) invites comparison with Henry Rogers. Both started building major railroads late in the game–1904. Both began with short lines to gain access to undeveloped coal seams—Rogers with the four mile Deepwater Railroad and Carter with the Lick Creek and Lake

Erie, some eight miles of road for transfer of coal from holdings near Dante, Virginia, to Fink near St. Paul, where the N&W's Norton branch could take it to market. Both attracted loyal and competent professional engineers and managers to advance their projects—Rogers with Thomas Nelson Page and Carter with M. J. Caples, "an operating man with an engineer's training," according to one who knew Carter well. Both had talents as entrepreneurs and could therefore attract venture capital. Rogers was an experienced hand on Wall Street, and although Carter was a rural Virginia "boy," he could attract both New York bankers and big-time developers of timber and coal in the Appalachians. Both hoped to reach coal markets in the Midwest and at ocean ports. Rogers succeeded in getting to Norfolk but not in getting to Toledo, where he owned lake front property. Carter wanted to go to Chicago and to reach the ocean via a harbor at the estuary of Cape Fear River at Southport, N. C. He did neither, but did achieve a valuable compromise.

Deciding like Rogers to expand his "satellite" road to a full fledged trunk line, Carter ended constructing a road linking the Big Sandy (important tributary of the Ohio) with the Piedmont region of South Carolina. It was not as hard as it sounded because ever since Charleston, South Carolina, had been a major American port on the Atlantic, the city fathers had sought a better inland connection than they had. A decline in Charleston's status as an Atlantic port in the 1830s made the leaders in Charleston to start turning their planning into action. A complex series of charters and surveys and some actual track laid the ground work for a route connecting Charleston with the Ohio Valley until the Civil War put an end to the projects. After the War, there were plans to put together the various bits and pieces of track that had been laid in North and South Carolina and Tennessee. Carter, a veteran coal developer, saw the projects coming together not as a gateway to Charleston, but as a freight and coal route connecting the Southeast with the Midwest by a direct route. As Ken Marsh wrote, "He clearly started the trans-mountain railroad project in 1902 with the first of a dozen or more corporations using the South and Western [Railroad] in various individual state corporate structures." Like Rogers, Carter wanted to keep his ambitious plans secret, so in order to be deliberately ambiguous he adopted the name "South and Western" and started linking together all the surveys and partially completed segments of the earlier 3-C Railroad. As Ken Marsh adds, "In 1905 Carter realized that he, unlike Rogers, could not finance the project himself. Thus, he attracted the New York firm of Blair & Company to finance the work." Both Carter and Rogers spared no expense in crossing, of necessity, every physiographic province in the southern Appalachian chain with a well engineered line consisting of strong bridges and

The Sewell seam of coal is 940 ft. above the C&O mainline and about 200 ft. from the top of the Plateau. Sewell, the settlement giving the seam its name, predated the arrival of the C&O main in the early 1870s. This occurred because a ferry operated over the New from 1806. Initially known as Bowyers' Ferry, by 1880 maps showed the community as Sewell Station. The coal train grinding upriver in 1957 passes Victorian styled station in area so remote that operator had to drive over coal mine road, park across the river, and walk in.

numerous tunnels with generous clearances. Both kept secret the rather audacious goals of the construction. And both expended much money on their projects, mostly due to crossing rugged landscapes directly. *Scientific American* in 1909 called the Carolina, Clinchfield, and Ohio "the costliest railroad in America," and Henry Rogers' death that year was in part due to the stress of completing the expensive road to Tidewater.

One dissimilarity was their backgrounds. Carter was no Easterner, like Kimball (from Philadelphia), or Rogers, from Massachusetts, or Huntington, from Connecticut. Carter was a mountain man, born in a small town on the edge of the Great Valley in southwest Virginia at the base of the Blue Ridge, some 40 miles, as the crow flies, from the nearest outcropping of the Pocahontas seam. From his first job, as clerk in in the old lead mines in Wythe County, Virginia, he acquired an interest in minerals and geology, an interest which was the foundation for such achievements as locating the important untapped seams in the "Trail of the Lonesome Pine" country of extreme southwest Virginia.

Having proved himself an astute business man in developing coal lands for the Virginia Coal and Iron Company and, as a subcontractor, in building part of the N&W's Clinch Valley extension (the Norton branch), Carter was able to attract New York bankers and outstanding Virginia timber developer William Ritter and Pocahontas coal operator I. T. Mann, to his

South and Western project. With Blair and Company controlling the Seaboard Air Line, Carter's next step was to build a connection south to the Seaboard, since the Southern by then controlled trackage intended for the connection with Charleston. Segments along the route to the southeast coast had already been built in unsuccessful attempts to complete a line from Charleston to the Ohio Valley. As historian Ron Eller wrote, "The main objective of the Clinchfield Railroad was to tap the coal reserves owned by the Blair interests and to provide for the transportation of that coal to the expanding textile mills of the southeast."

Construction south from Dante, Virginia, across Tennessee and the Blue Ridge barrier was difficult. But the earth moving that the line required was getting an impetus from the determination of the United States, around this time, to complete the Panama Canal, a job the French had given up. Also, M. J. Caples became general manager and chief engineer of Carter's South and Western. As such, he prevailed upon Carter to build the road to very high standards. In the words of retired chief engineer J. A. Goforth, "The Clinchfield was built to construction standards far beyond the norms of the time. Consequently, Clinchfield has not had to reduce grades, lighten curves, enlarge tunnels and strengthen bridges to carry present day traffic as other railroads have had to do." The Virginian Railway also had been constructed through very rugged country with equally

The old Blue Ridge tunnel mouth, part of which can be seen above the middle of the first E8 locomotive unit, attests to just how long ago C&O was founded, though its name then was the Virginia Central. *The Sportsman*, eastbound, is emerging in the 1960s from the newer and longer Tunnel, completed in 1942. The older tunnel, at 4263 ft., was something of an engineering marvel in 1857. During the Civil War the tunnel was used for troop movements in and out of the Great Valley of Virginia, as for example, when Stonewall Jackson's men moved in several train loads out of the Valley to disembark at a station short of Richmond in order to help stop McClelland's advance on Richmond in 1862.

high standards, and again those high standards were enforced by the influence of an engineer very close to Rogers—William N. Page.

Some three years after completion of the Clinchfield route to Spartansburg, SC, which became its southern terminus, Carter decided to build north, for a connection with the Ohio River was what early proponents of a railroad in this region had always wanted. A real engineering problem presented itself just north of Dante in the form of a mountain named Sandy Ridge, part of the escarpment called the "Allegheny Front," extending from southeastern Tennessee nearly to New York state. This ridge marked the eastern edge of the Appalachian Plateau and the start of the Valley and Ridge Province. It is the same ridge that the N&W tunnels through at Great Flattop Mountain, the Virginian at Clarks Gap, and farther north, the B&O at Sand Patch and the Pennsylvania Railroad at Gallitzen. To keep the maximum mainline grade on the Clinchfield at 1.5% required a tunnel through the solid rock of Sandy Ridge 7,854 ft. long. Construction to a connection with the C&O at Elkhorn City, Ky., was completed in 1915. The so-called Elkhorn extension had been locat-

ed by Carter as early as 1902 in the critical area around the Breaks of the Big Sandy just south of Elkhorn City, Ky. The area was critical because Chesapeake and Ohio was in a race with the Clinchfield to get a right-of-way surveyed through the narrow gorge and also because of the difficulty of surveying past steep rock cliffs bordering a narrow stream.

Carter, perhaps the most eccentric of the four men developing trans-Appalachian railroads, was also the most restless, and in 1916 he had the audacity to give up his interests in the Clinchfield and to develop coal lands in the heart of the McDowell County, West Virginia, already at that time the leading coal producing county in West Virginia! It appears he sank a shaft down to Pocahontas seam no. 4, the famous no. 3 seam below it apparently being too difficult at that point to mine. His mine at Coalwood became a top producer, despite his having to deal with drainage problems caused by the shaft method of mining. Here again he constructed a feeder line, the West Virginia Southwestern Railroad, to connect with Norfolk and Western, which in time the Norfolk and Western absorbed.

County on Elkhorn Creek is named for him. (Kimball's predecessor, William Mahone, of course, was the real founder of the N&W. His reign was too early, however, for him to know that N&W's future lay with coal. Whether he loved nature is open to question, but as the Confederate general who turned disaster into "victory" at the Battle of the Crater at Petersburg, he was certainly colorful, and a life-sized statue of him overlooks the remains of the crater today.) Henry H. Rogers had a winning personality and was known as the "handsomest man on Wall Street." Friend of Mark Twain and noted philanthropist, he took the press and coal operators on a proud "owner's" tour of the Virginian shortly after its completion. (He was aboard his private car, *Dixie*, built in 1906, later donated to the Kentucky Railway Museum, now gone.) That he actually liked the mountains of Kanawha, Fayette, and Monroe counties, where his railroad originated, is attested to by the name of his luxurious yacht– the *Kanawha*. Alas, in 1909 he died shortly after his monumental railroad was completed to Norfolk.

George L. Carter looks good with his full moustache (a decoration he and Rogers shared), but by all accounts he was a very private man who would

One of the goals of this book is to link this group of four coal carrying railroads with the physiographic regions they tapped and passed through. This comparison invites examining the human sides of the four "captains of industry" who made sure their railroads exploited and "conquered" the region. It is true that the photographs in this book place a romantic aura around both the railroads and the countryside the rails passed through. Can one find any evidence that the hard-headed businessmen who oversaw these enterprises were ever in touch with the beauties of nature? We do know that C. P. Huntington by the simple act of going to California in 1849 via the Isthmus of Panama liked to "rough it." We also know that on completion of the CP over Sierra Nevada, he commissioned a well known painter of American Western scenery to paint the tracks at Donner summit of the Cascades–and took the artist there in his private car. And he was at his summer home on Lake Raquette in the rugged Adirondacks when he died. Frederick Kimball was so low key as a CEO that he left few indications about how he felt on completing a line to the Pocahontas field. He does have one link with nature—a small town in McDowell

rather travel in a day coach, where he could preserve his anonymity, than in his private car where he would be on display. His biographer in *Virginia Cavalcade* adds that he even "forbade his own newspaper, the *Bristol Herald Courier*, ever to print his name." Like most captains of industry at the turn of the century (before the income tax that came with World War I) he gave freely of his money to regional charities and educational causes. Since as a private man he kept no diaries and since his wife, unlike Libby Custer, did not care to write about him after his death, we know little of what Carter saw in nature. But we do have an image of him in his knee-high boots, riding a sure-footed mule, climbing cliffs and trudging through dark woods, scraping the leaves away on a gentle slope in order to measure the thickness of an exposed coal seam—an image which shows him as belonging with the Appalachian highlands and not an alien trespassing there. This image conforms to an interesting photo in James A. Goforth's *Building the Clinchfield*. Dated 1905, the picture shows ten men, each mounted on a fine steed and each dressed in formal businessmen's attire of the times. They are lined facing the camera with George Carter himself, erect and looking at home in the saddle, at one end of the column. In the background is a fairly large coal tipple of the times with a coal car under it. Labeled "the syndicate that backed the construction of the S&W and C C & O," they are obviously men of means who are happy to be roughing it and to show off their equestrian talents. And Carter is obviously happy to be selling the men his new road.

How did these four roads end up? The transition of C&O into Chessie and into CSX and N&W into Norfolk Southern is rather well known, even down to the fight of the two roads over possession of Conrail. The Virginian was the first to lose its identity. For a long time the ICC had been unwilling to approve mergers of parallel and competing lines, which is what N&W and Virginian were. In fact, in 1948 the ICC turned down C&O's Chairman of the board Robert Young's bid for the Virginian for that very reason. But ten years later railroad monopolies were no longer considered a threat to the nation's economic well being. Therefore, in 1959 the ICC approved N&W's takeover of its rich Pocahontas coal field competitor. That made the N&W more of a force in eastern railroading than ever. With twin port facilities at Norfolk and twin yards at Roanoke and twin lines up the New River between Glen Lyn and Radford, plus closely paralleling lines clear across Virginia, the new N&W was able to achieve great savings in operations. The Clinchfield maintained an identity until the 1980s, when it became part of CSX. Though it still was a route for coal moving south and to some extent north, its main loss of identity was as a first-class route for perishables moving out of Georgia and Florida and South Carolina to industrial centers of the north, most notably Detroit. This had been a joint operation involving the Seaboard, the Charleston and Western Carolina, the Piedmont and Northern, the Clinchfield, and the C&O's route from Elkhorn City up the Big Sandy to the Ohio and thence across Ohio to Toledo and via the Pere Marquette (until its merger with C&O in 1947) into Detroit. And Donald Traser, in his *Virginia Railway Depots* has uncovered an interesting "Believe It Or Not" fact about the Clinchfield: "Within its 277 miles it operates in five states– Kentucky, Virginia, Tennessee, and North and South Carolina. No other railroad in the United States operates in so many states in so short a distance."

C&O Ry Photo/C&O Historical Society Collection
Industrial photographer William Ritasse covered C&O in 1944. Scouting the New River gorge for locations, he found the Lovers' Leap overlook, near Hawk's Nest, well suited to the *Machine in the Garden* motif in which a harmony exists between industrial progress and bucolic tranquility. Today, the overlook is fenced in and a cable car descends from the Resort to an anchor located about where the building is. In 1944, access was difficult! Cliff is formed by Lower Nuttall sandstone, and train is down river headed by a 2-6-6-6.

> ... The hills
> Rock-ribbed and ancient as the sun,—
> ... The venerable woods—rivers that move
> In majesty, and the complaining brooks...
>
> —William Cullen Bryant

ailroads, Appalachian history and Appalachian scenery make an appealing tripartite unity. Probably the four locales best illustrating this unity are the Hudson River just north of West Point, New York, the confluence of the Shenandoah and Potomac Rivers at Harpers Ferry, W.Va., the view from Lookout Mountain in Tennessee and the prospect of Cumberland Gap as seen from the National Park.

Truly sublime is the spot above West Point, where the wide and placid Hudson flows between the brows of four looming mountains–Storm King, Crow's Nest, Break Neck and Bull Hill (together forming a northern extension of the Blue Ridge Province). Here was a fortress in Revolutionary War days keeping the British from sailing up to Albany, and here on both sides of the river were busy "water level" lines of the New York Central (now CSX and Metro North). Southwest of the Hudson Highlands was the rugged gorge of the rock-strewn Potomac, cutting through the Blue Ridge barrier and providing a path (albeit one requiring a tunnel through a cliff hanging above the river) for the Baltimore and Ohio (now CSX). Harpers Ferry was of course, not only the place where abolitionist John Brown stormed the federal arsenal, it was also a key position in the struggle of Union and Confederate armies for control of the Great Valley. At the south end of the Appalachian chain one looks down from a park atop Lookout Mountain, locale of the "Battle Above the Clouds" in the Civil War, upon the vista far below of the city of Chattanooga, the Cumberland Plateau, and Moccasin Bend of the Tennessee River, where the Southern (now NS) winds along its banks below the viewer. And one can't forget Daniel Boone, leading the band of settlers down the Powell Valley and thence into the "happy hunting grounds" of what would be the state of Kentucky through a break in the wall of the Cumberlands known, of course, as Cumberland Gap. (The wall is an escarpment, known north of the Cumberlands as the "Allegheny Front.") Today one can see CSX and NS tunnel under the Gap (a wind gap) while visiting the National Historical Park at the Gap. One could continue with nominations for this

"unity." For example, there is the vista near Fort Ticonderoga, New York, where the "Green Mountain Boys" fought, and where between the Fort and Lake Champlain the mainline of the Delaware and Hudson (now Canadian Pacific) runs.

Another unity in the study of the Appalachians' relationship to railroading is how the physiographic provinces comprising the Appalachian chain form an identical pattern in the crossing of the mountains by all four roads. (In nature there are of course, anomalies, so "identical" must be used cautiously.) These provinces are from west to east: the Appalachian Plateau, Ridge and Valley Province, the Great Valley, and the Blue Ridge.

The Appalachian Plateau (called Cumberland Plateau south of eastern Kentucky) looks level, like a plain, if viewed from high enough angle that reveals how level the top usually is despite deep dissection of the plateau's surface by steams that look like veins in a leaf if viewed from the air. Hence the description "dendridic" drainage. Those green-muffled West Virginia hills, then, are not really hills; they are valleys (at least until one comes to the Ridge and Valley Province in the extreme eastern part of the state). Three exceptions to a level top surface, denoting a plain at one time, are: (1) a particularly resistant rock layer that causes an elevation noticeable above the surface of the plain (like Flat Top Mountain); (2) the existence of a preglacial river bed (called the Teays in West Virginia) above the level of the Ohio (a base level for drainage) and below the level of the plain (called a peneplain); (3) a "great fault block thrust northwestward" (citing Fenneman) marking the border between Kentucky and Virginia and creating Pine Mountain.

Viewed close-up, the distinguishing characteristic of the entire Plateau is the bedding of the rocks and their composition. Mostly, the bedding is horizontal, with "faults" sometimes causing displacement in the bedding. The rocks are all sedimentary, made up mostly of layers of sandstone, shale, coal, conglomerates, and limestone (and its kindred rock, dolomite). Some sandstones are harder and thicker than other

Camera aimed south in August 1988 catches a CSX coal train, bound for Columbus on former C&O tracks, crossing the Pickaway Plains north of Chillicothe. Conical hill in background is Mt. Logan, featured on Great Seal of Ohio.

Glacial deposits known as end moraines characterize the general area north of Chillicothe along U.S. 23. "This general area also is the boundary between two major physiographic provinces—the Central Lowland to the north and west and the Appalachian Plateau to the south and east. This boundary is marked by bedrock hills that are especially prominent to the east of Route 23. The line of hills that suddenly rise from the gentle glaciated topography is termed the Allegheny escarpment and marks the eastern edge of the Great Plains..."

— pamphlet, *Guide to the Geology Along U. S. 23*, Ohio Dept. of Natural Resources

Simple articulated N&W 1234, highballing long train of empty coal cars back to coal fields, is amid the hills of the Appalachian Plateau (near Franklin Furnace, Ohio) yet it might as well be running across flat prairies, for the civil engineers who laid out the route made sure the tracks followed the flood plain of the Ohio and its tributaries. The only problems with such a "bottoms land" route are indirection and periodic flooding (which the U.S. government mostly licked with flood control dams).

sandstones; therefore, some sandstones, being more resistant to weathering, form higher and more massive cliffs.

The borders of this province are much more easily delineated on the eastern edge than on the western. That is mainly because the level of the plateau on the western side is lower than on the eastern. That is, the plateau slopes gradually upward toward the southeast, so that to an observer the hills get higher and higher as he travels southeast. The eastern border of the Plateau is an escarpment named the Allegheny Front (see below). Only the N&W and C&O (before they became NS and CSX respectively) crossed the Plateau completely. Both originated in the Central Lowlands (meaning Cincinnati and Chicago) and both had major coal lines extending to Columbus and farther north. On the lines to Cincinnati the demarcation between the Provinces is not pronounced. However, because the great glaciers that extended south through Ohio to just south of Columbus flattened the landscape, there is a clear boundary on the west edge of the Plateau. In fact, a "hill" at the boundary just north of Chillicothe became the hill behind the field of grain on the seal of the state of Ohio. The Virginian and Clinchfield both began in the middle of the province where the hills are getting higher. Three of the four roads extend beyond the Plateau and through the Ridge and Valley Province to the Great Valley, the Blue Ridge, into the Piedmont Province and beyond to the Atlantic Coastal Plain. (The Clinchfield terminated in the Piedmont at Spartansburg, South Carolina.)

The passage of the Clinchfield through the Plateau Province at one place along the Russell Fork of the Big Sandy is so unusual as to have inspired the states of Virginia and Kentucky to create a joint park in the area. Here, one can enjoy the scenery where the river and railroad encounter the Breaks of the Big Sandy. Pine Mountain forms the Breaks and on its summit is the state line. The huge overthrust fault forming the mountain ridge has raised a resistant sandstone layer "on edge" so to speak, requiring the Russell Fork to cut through it in a gorge some 5 miles long, averaging 1,000 ft. in depth and having steep sides and narrow, rocky bottom, plus interesting tunnels and bridges for the Clinchfield. The highway and park are far above the level of railroad and river.

E. L. Huddleston

Looking north as extra 6717 enters the Central Lowlands, one sees across U.S. 23 evidence of glaciation in the leveled landscape, including end moraine marked by hummocky rises on the skyline.

The Allegheny Front, while not a province, is a physiographic feature with such pronounced effect on railroad location and operation that it deserves separate treatment. The Writers' Project, *Guide to West Virginia*, describes this feature in that state: "The state is divided into two physiographic provinces by an escarpment known as the Allegheny Front, which extends in an irregular line from Keyser, on the West-Virginia-Maryland boundary, south-westward to Bluefield on the Virginia-West Virginia line. East of the Front is the Appalachian Valley and Ridge Province." North of West Virginia and Maryland, into Pennsylvania, the Front makes for operating problem on all railroads crossing it. Since the Front is like a wall with few passes through it, the great Pennsylvania Railroad attacked the wall by detouring up a side ridge and reversing direction with a horseshoe curve. This permitted climbing the slope without an excessive grade, which was kept to 1.8%, though a relatively short tunnel was required under the brow of the Front at Gallitzin. Farther south the B&O's Baltimore-Chicago main line penetrated the wall, after a climb up historic Wills Creek, with a long tunnel and a 2.25% grade. And in the same area, the Western Maryland (now abandoned) crested the Front at Deal, Pennsylvania, 3,060 ft above sea level, the highest main line crossing in the whole Appalachian chain. Farther south, the B&O's famous Seventeen-Mile grade (now CSX) ascends the Front from the east and the equally famous Cranberry grade from the west.

E. L. Huddleston
The Ohio River, from Pittsburgh to near Louisville, flows between high hills of the Appalachian Plateau and the Cincinnati Arch, with a flood plain that varies in width. Allegheny type 1623 heads 160 coal loads for Columbus.

Chesapeake and Ohio, the only major road that crossed the Allegheny Front without having to climb it, followed the New River eastward. Actually, a very old river formed before the uplift that created the Plateau and the Front, the New cut through the Front, in an area where there is an anomaly concerning the location of the "wall." Causing this anomaly is a shift to the west of the Front and the existence of two rivers, the New and its tributary, the Greenbrier, which cause a discontinuity in its location. From one point of view, the C&O passes the Allegheny Front at the east portal of Big Bend Tunnel. Looming above and behind this portal is the summit of Keeneys Knob, with an altitude consistent with high elevations of the Front north of the Greenbrier and south of it. On the other hand, C&O can also be said to leave the Plateau Province when it crosses the Greenbrier at the point this scenic river veers north conforming to a trellis drainage pattern of the bordering Valley and Ridge Province. Where the Virginian and Norfolk and Western cross the Front is also ambiguous. The tunnel under Great Flattop Mountain

on the N&W and the short tunnel on the Virginian at Clarks Gap both are at the highest elevation of the Plateau in southeastern West Virginia and are near its eastern edge. Thus, they should mark the Front in that area.

Whether one considers the Front to be the summit of Flattop Mountain or farther east along the boundary with the Ridge and Valley Province, one thing is clear–the Front does abut on the Ridge and Valley Province in the vicinity of Bluefield. Instead of a wide valley separating the Front from the westernmost "folded" ridge, the two are almost piled up one upon the other. From Bluefield to Glen Lyn, the N&W and Virginian follow steeply downgrade the declivity formed by the meeting of East River Mountain with the "Front" of the Appalachian Plateau. At Glen Lyn, on the border between Virginia and West Virginia and on the border between the two provinces, the Virginian and N&W enter the New River valley as that steam cuts south through the Ridge and Valley Province, beginning at Narrows, Va.

The Clinchfield Railroad passes through the

Allegheny Front just north of Dante (pronounced Dant) Virginia, via an 7854 ft. tunnel named Sandy Ridge, said to be the tenth longest in the United States. To get from Dante to the Tunnel–a little over a mile–required a grade of 1.8%. South of West Virginia the Plateau and its front are named Cumberland. The Cumberland Mountains of course extend into Kentucky. Construction of the so called Elkhorn Extension of the Clinchfield through the Plateau Province was put off because of the construction difficulty posed by the Cumberland Front at Dante as well as by the narrow canyon and rock formations at the Breaks.

The description of the Valley and Ridge Province given in Federal Writers' Project Guide to West Virginia is apt for the entire region: "The drainage of this portion of West Virginia...is of the trellis pattern characteristic of such strongly folded areas. Weathering and erosion have etched into bold relief...[the folded and upturned] massive sandstone strata and at the same time have created valleys in the weaker limestones and shales. In this manner, parallel ridges and valleys have been formed, with a general northeast-southwest trend. Some streams flow in a trough or valley for 40 or 50 miles, cross a ridge through a water gap, and then resume the original direction in a parallel valley." "Folding" is somewhat misleading for the major ridges. Because the remnants of huge folds are left standing as parallel ridges of practically uniform height, "turned at angles" would be more apt than folding for describing the layering of the mostly sedimentary rocks. In West Virginia and northwestern Virginia the main "level" ridges are typically four in number with the Province being thirty to forty miles wide. These ridges of course have names which loom large in the geography of the region—e.g., North Mountain, Peters Mountain, East River Mountain, Big Walker, Potts.

E. L. Huddleston
The almost level surface of the Appalachian Plateau is apparent in the line of hills in Ohio as C&O 2-8-4 2759 heads up the Ohio at Catlettsburg, Ky., in 1953. Train of Virginian empty coal cars will leave the Ohio at Huntington and head down the Guyandotte to Logan.

For much of the length of the eastern border of West Virginia with Virginia the watershed between the Gulf of Mexico and the Atlantic Ocean is formed by one of these ridges, named Alleghany Mountain in the area where the C&O main line crosses the watershed in a nearly mile long tunnel. The old Virginian and the N&W had parallel lines through the Valley and Ridge Province that followed the New River through the Province. Hence, both have very scenic routes with huge ridges, like Big Walker Mountain, rising above and behind the immediate river valley, which is bordered by dolomite cliffs in some fantastic shapes. Near the southeastern edge of the Province both roads climb upgrade out of the New River Valley and across a divide (via tunnels) before descending into the Roanoke basin. At the divide within the Ridge and Valley Province, near the city of Christiansburg, Virginia, is the Atlantic-Gulf watershed. The Clinchfield crosses the Valley, and Ridge Province at a point where there is only one major "folded" ridge—Clinch Mountain—that rises above a

mostly limestone plateau. There are other parallel ridges in the area, but mostly they are "buried" and show relatively little relief to differentiate them from the surrounding countryside. (Powell Mountain becomes a major ridge several miles southwest of where the Clinchfield Railroad crosses the Province.) There is little physically to mark the passage of the CRR into the Great Valley, other than its emergence from a tunnel under Clinch Mountain.

The Great Valley is easily identified on a map of the eastern United States by the path of Interstate Highway 81 from Harrisburg, Pa. to its junction with INT 40 and beyond into Knoxville. In that distance it is safe to say the highway never leaves the Valley. If valley is defined as a depression following the path of a stream, then Great Valley is not a valley. True, parts of the long "valley" have streams conforming to its southwest trend; e.g., the Shenandoah River, but the main identifier of the Valley is that it is bordered by the eastern most ridge of the Ridge and Valley Province and on its east side by the mass of the Blue

E. L. Huddleston

A classically proportioned class H-6 Mallet, on mine run assignment in 1955, has "hostler" at the throttle in the now abandoned Handley yards on the upper Kanawha where evidence of the upward slope of the Appalachian Plateau is seen in the increasingly higher West Virginia hills.

Ridge Province. Where the valley is narrow enough one can be in the middle of the Valley and see high mountains clearly on each side. In an area of south-western Virginia where the C&O's James River line crosses the Valley, at Buchanan, the two Provinces come almost together. Where the Valley Province is twenty or so miles wide, the gradient profile of rail-roads crossing it can be quite jagged, since the Valley topography has humps and depressions, depending on the rock structures, which are mostly metamor-phosed sedimentary rocks. The Clinchfield Railroad crosses the Valley roughly between Kingsport and Johnson City, Tennessee.

The eastern most mountain range in the central Appalachians is known as the Blue Ridge. And this name applies to the Province extending from the Great Smokies to Harrisburg, Pennsylvania. The Blue Ridge forms a beautiful mountain range, for in much of its extent the range has only one major ridge and the summits are irregular, unlike the mostly uniform ridges of the Ridge and Valley section. The Blue Ridge Parkway and its northern extension, the Shenandoah National Park, take advantage of the scenic splen-dors—to the west the Great Valley and beyond that the Ridge and Valley Province and to the east, at usu-ally a considerably lower elevation than the Great

The New River, like no other river, cuts through the entire Appalachian chain. Rising in the North Carolina Blue Ridge, it flows across the Great Valley, cuts through the Ridge and Valley province, and creates a deep gorge in the Appalachian Plateau before joining with the Kanawha. Building westward, C&O used the New River Gorge and the N&W and Virginian used the river's passage through the ridges of the Ridge and Valley Province to avoid a roundabout path through that province.

Valley, the Piedmont Province, with its "foothills" of the main Blue Ridge (e.g., the "little mountain" that Thomas Jefferson's house sits on). These mountains are composed of metamorphic with some Precambrian, the oldest rocks on the continent, which are complex in structure and bedding.

The four Pocahontas roads cross the Blue Ridge in scenes of splendor. The C&O was fortunate enough (from an esthetic but not from an operational viewpoint) to cross the Blue Ridge twice. On its Mountain Subdivision, the original route through Virginia, the C&O, heading west, climbs the slope of the Blue Ridge west of Crozet, Virginia, and passes

Mountain Grades

Unbeatable for evoking the "romance" of railroading are heavy trains on steep grades, and this combination was the forte of the Pocahontas roads. Each had to contend with grades against the movement of loaded coal cars, but ranked according to the difficulty the grades imposed on operations, the Virginian was probably first, Norfolk and Western second, the Clinchfield third, and Chesapeake and Ohio fourth. With big enough train load, say 100 loaded 100-ton coal cars, the grade does not have to be very steep to set up an operational obstacle. In fact, on an ascending grade of one percent (that is, a one foot rise in 100 ft.) a locomotive can pull only about one-fifth the tonnage which it can keep rolling on straight and level track. Put another way, a one percent grade quadruples normal resistance of the trailing load. And whether the train ever has to stop on the grade or near its start must be factored in. If the train can keep on moving, it can probably surmount the grade with its kinetic energy aiding the energy of the locomotive, assuming the train has not lost its momentum. As John Armstrong writes, "Energy in a train going 60 mph is enough to lift its weight 115 ft., so a short incline may be run as a 'momentum grade.'"

The speed at which a locomotive can take a given load up a grade becomes important in determining operations on that grade. A grade significantly slows a heavy train. A train powered at 1.5 horsepower per ton, which could make 60 mph on level track, will slow to about 22 mph on a grade of one percent and to 10 mph on two percent. A sustained grade of one percent even presents a problem to a train descending it, for the same dead weight resisting movement in the uphill struggle becomes kinetic energy on the downhill. Just as the increasing efficiency of diesel-electrics alleviated operating problems on sustained ascending grades, so has dynamic braking on diesels speeded up downhill tonnage moves. Fifty years ago a coal train descending a long grade would be delayed by turning up the retainers at the top of the grade and turning them down at the bottom. (The 26L locomotive brake valve would have a pressure maintaining feature, eliminating the stops.) In addition, the speed limit down the hill was apt to be lower than necessary as a safety feature, and braking meant considerable wear on brake shoes. They became so hot that on coal trains of that era heat would burn away some of the friction-bearing journal box oil that had caked on the wheel, causing blue smoke to rise from under the descending coal cars. With dynamic braking the heat generated by brake shoes is nil and the oil in roller-bearing journal boxes is sealed inside. Thus no smoke.

Another factor affecting the resistance of cars on grades is the presence of curves, which naturally add to the pull. Even on level track, an 8 degree curve, for example, will double the resistance of all cars on the curve. (Put another way, each degree of curvature adds to the resistance of the train almost one pound per ton of trailing weight.) A reverse, or "S" curve, is a double whammy. And in Appalachia adjoining "S" curves are common enough, especially in track locations conforming to mountainside slopes or along winding streams. Track work itself affects operation on grades. Thus superelevating, or "banking" curves (raising the outer rail a maximum of 6 inches) can ease the pressure of the inner flange against the rail. A major advancement in track laying was devising a way to lay rail in continuous lengths of about 1500 ft. Until the 1970s, when welded rail came in wide use, the standard rail length was was 39 ft. (Forty ft. was the length of gondolas transporting rail.) Eliminating the wear and battering at the end of the 39 ft. rail sections not only cut maintenance costs but decreased friction between rail and wheel, something that could be visibly confirmed by noting the smoothness of the rolling coal cars on welded rail, plus how well welded rail cut down noise of the moving cars.

Sources: John H. Armstrong, *The Railroad–What It Is, What It Does* (Simmons-Boardman, 1977); Robert S. Henry, *This Fascinating Railroad Business* (Indianapolis, Bobbs-Merrill, 1946).

---

under the summit at Rockfish Gap by a long tunnel and thence into the Great Valley. The Amtrak *Cardinal* still runs over this pre-Civil War and very scenic route. To the south C&O's main freight line, following the Jackson and James rivers from the Ridge and Valley section through to the ocean, is able to penetrate the Blue Ridge barrier by following the banks of the James, for the James cuts a "water gap" through the mountain mass just east of Balcony Falls. (The gap at Rockfish is known as a Wind Gap.). Still father south in Old Virginia, the Norfolk and Western main line cuts through the Blue Ridge via a wind gap that so reduces the height of the mountain barrier just east of the city that a tunnel is not required. The Virginian was even more fortunate. It paralleled the N&W across the Ridge and Valley and into the Great Valley and thence into city of Roanoke, where the N&W was on the north side and Virginian on the south side. The civil engineers locating the Virginian were able to survey even less a grade for getting their new (1907) line across the Blue Ridge barrier. It used the water gap formed by the Roanoke River, but since

E.L. Huddleston

Though abandoned by the time of this picture in 1966, the Keeneys Creek switchback is still visible on the north slope of the gorge. The old Nuttall drift mine taps the Sewell seam with a long enclosed conveyor extending up the mountain. Behind it, about halfway up, is the switch at the tail track for the switchback. A coal train, on the south side, heads east up the river past track to the Kaymoor mine, long abandoned.

that river veered farther south once past the Blue Ridge than seemed warranted in terms of mileage, the new line proceeded up a 0.2% grade away from the river to a low divide between the Roanoke and its northern tributary, Goose Creek, which it descended on a 0.6 grade into the Piedmont Province, which offered no further mountains to cross and mostly a gradual downward grade toward Tidewater.

The Clinchfield (now CSX) had by far the most spectacular crossing of the Blue Ridge Province. Col. Fred Olds' reaction, after riding over the line in 1908, was apt: "The run was densely bordered with

W. H. O'Dell

Though C&O's main line does not have to climb the Appalachian Plateau to get through it, C&O's coal branches in the New River field did. Such was the Keeneys Creek Subdivision, which gained altitude by means of a switchback along the slope of the gorge above the mainline (which featured one main track on each side of the river). This 1953 photo looks west at the branch starting up the mountain. Track will head in reverse direction at the tail track of switchback, halfway up the mountainside, and proceed up Keeneys Creek.

In this March, 2000, view the Keeneys Creek branch has been so long abandoned that one has to look carefully about half way up the mountain at left to see two of the bridges carrying the branch up Keeneys Creek. Below, the Amtrak *Cardinal* runs east toward Washington

Rhododendron. We had traveled all the way from Marion [North Carolina] along a route fringed with this noblest of all mountain flowers and hence the title of the 'Rhododendron Route' is peculiarly fitting." One reason for its awesomeness was that the Province in that part of Tennessee-North Carolina spreads beyond just one narrow main range to include a jumble of ridges, which are often over a mile high. Mount Mitchell, highest mountain east of the Mississippi, was within sight of the Clinchfield mainline. On top of that, the railroad climbed the long steep eastward slope of the Blue Ridge via a series of four loops making up a single larger loop that kept the ascending grade at a constant 1.2% but which required 17 tunnels in 11 miles, including the 1865 ft. tunnel at the very summit, naturally named Blue Ridge. At this point is the Atlantic-Mississippi watershed for the Clinchfield.

At one point the topmost loop is so near the line farther down the mountain that they were only 1.9 miles apart, but measured by rail distance they were 16! The best way for an individual to take in this spectacle is from an overlook on the Blue Ridge Parkway that surveys the whole scene. If that was not enough, the track descends from the summit of the Blue Ridge at Altapass northward toward the Great Valley via an eight-mile long gorge of the Nolichucky River along which the railroad barely had room for a single track that often had to be shored up by concrete retaining walls because there was no river bank to lay tracks on. That early traveler, Col. Olds, made clear how the gorge was subject to both slides and floods: "Pile upon pile of rock the cliffs rose, now sloping sharply, now almost perpendicular, all stone with stunted trees...This Toe or Nolichucky River is treacherous in the extreme and seven years ago rose 52 feet in this gorge. It took away 16 miles of the railroad, and it required some months to replace it."

Left: New River gorge seen from Cunard, looking upriver at eastbound CSX grain train, March 5, 2000. Double track mainline diverges at Sewell bridge and will come together at Hawks Nest. Abandoned Mann's Creek narrow gauge is on flank of mountain facing camera, about half way up.

Bottom: Eastbound loaded coal train grinds slowly upgrade across Sewell bridge, September 1957. Camera faces mountainside near Cunard from which photo of grain train was taken some 43 years later.

These locomotives, fresh from major shopping at Huntington, are headed east to Charlottesville in 1948 to work on the Washington and Virginia Air Line Subdivisions. In the lead is a class B-1 2-10-2, followed by an H-5 2-6-6-2 built by the United States Railroad Administration. At Hinton, near the Allegheny Front, the Appalachian Plateau is at its highest.

At west portal of mile long Big Bend Tunnel, class J-1 4-8-2, no. 540, the first Mountain type built, brings local down-grade through the old bore in 1947. Before par-allel bore was drilled in 1932, the old tunnel had to be ventilated with two blowers housed in this structure, forcing smoke east out of tunnel ahead of engine passing through it. The tunnels avoided a long bend in the Greenbrier River, a spot which for all practi-cal purposes marks the Allegheny Front.

C&O extra east at Alderson, W.Va., follows Greenbrier River east through limestone plateau country marking border between the Appalachian Plateau, whose "front" is seen in the long ridge in background, and the folded Alleghenies, which begin when the railroad leaves the Greenbrier beyond Ronceverte. Prominence on the ridge above the locomotive is Keeneys Knob, 4100 ft. in elevation.

Pusher on this coal train, two miles east of White Sulphur Springs in June 1951, nears the main divide of the Ridge and Valley Province, where water on one side of the ridge drains to the Atlantic and on the other to the Gulf. The dividing ridge, visible in the top right background, is also the border between Virginia and West Virginia.

E. L. Huddleston

Pusher engine 1624, pictured above, has gone under the dividing ridge with its train by way of Alleghany (twin) tunnels and is now at Alleghany, Virginia, summit of the folded Alleghenies. 1624 will turn and head back to Hinton light.

E. L. Huddleston

Two miles east of the Alleghany summit, C&O crosses Jerrys Run on a huge fill (behind photographer) and then follows the Run before curving east as the stream heads toward Dunlap Creek, far below, flowing between two long parallel ridges of the Ridge and Valley Province. EMD F7s are westbound up the Allegheny slope December, 1957.

From Clifton Forge, on the Jackson River, the C&O had two "main" lines across Virginia–the Mountain Sub-Division leading toward Washington and the James River line (which began as a canal) allowing a water-level route (albeit a rather crooked one) to Tidewater.

E. L. Huddleston

The Mountain Sub-Division local freight heads across the Great Valley west of Staunton, August 1958. Against the horizon is the easternmost long ridge of the Ridge and Valley Province. Rising as a Monadnock (prominence) is Elliott Knob, over 4200 ft. elevation, part of ridge known as Great North Mountain, in front of which is Little North Mountain. In between is Buffalo Gap, which the local passed some nine miles back.

William E. Warden, Jr.
Above: In the evening of a summer day, 1969, the westbound *George Washington* starts across the Great Valley, with city of Waynesboro in background, and beyond it the mass of the Blue Ridge at Rockfish Gap, which the train had tunneled under some four and a half miles back.

E. L. Huddleston
Left: East of Big Island, Virginia, on C&O's James River line to Tidewater, the local freight hurries east, August, 1961. About seven miles back is the main mass of the Blue Ridge, through which the river cuts a gap near Balcony Falls.

At junction of the "Peavine" (line to Cincinnati) with N&W's double track line up the Scioto (on which photographer is standing), 4-8-4 no. 604 brings the eastbound *Cavalier* toward Portsmouth, July 11, 1953. In background is the Appalachian Plateau. Scenic hills line both sides of the valley as far north as Chillicothe. Most unusual is the nine truss spans over a river for which two would seem enough.

Below: At this important main line junction, a manifest off the Peavine, headed by 2-8-8-2 no. 2105, heads toward Portsmouth on the same day that photographer Acton shot the *Cavalier*.

Right: By December, 1958, the job of the articulated class A 2-6-6-4s has been taken over largely by diesels, like this long train of empties headed for Wiiliamson along the Tug Fork behind two Geeps. Behind the train order office at Kermit, W.Va., is Y-6a 2166, taking lunch. After extra 621 clears, 2166 will pull loads at coal mines near Warfield, Ky. Two sandstone "buttes" on the surface of the peneplain (Appalachian Plateau) on distant horizon are most unusual.

E. L. Huddleston

Through a West Virginia coal camp near Naugatuck on the Tug Fork of the Big Sandy, a 190 car coal train, headed by articulated class A no. 1209, works full throttle through the many twists and turns of the crooked river on its way to Portsmouth in 1957. Rivers and creeks provide the only feasible rail routes into and out of the Appalachian Plateau province.

Gary E. Huddleston

Above: On this particular run in 1959, tonnage had been reduced at Farm to 87 cars, and extra 2183 charges up Elkhorn Creek with Alco diesel pushers. About to enter one of the twin tunnels near Kimball (see photo page 29), engineer S. R. Scott is working full throttle but has not yet opened the "booster valve" that gives a burst of high pressure steam to the low pressure front engine. Fireman has crossed gangway to see photographers that engineer has told him about.

E.L. Huddleston

Top Right: As the Appalachian Plateau tilts upward, the grade along the Tug Fork gets increasingly steeper—steep enough to require a pusher, like this Y6b (with caboose coupled behind auxiliary tender) pushing near Roderfield. At Farm, the train's tonnage will be cut for the climb up Elkhorn Creek to Elkhorn Tunnel under Great Flattop Mountain. N&W 2-8-8-2s powered practically all freight trains over coal rich Pocahontas Division.

Wally Johnson

Right: Through a tunnel made necessary by the crooked Tug Fork, a train of empty coal cars headed by one of the ubiquitous N&W 2-8-8-2s, coasts downgrade near Roderfield in 1954.

Both: Gary E. Huddleston

Left: You'd better believe engineer Scott has turned on the booster; there's no other way to account for the uninterrupted and voluminous cascade of smoke and steam that mark the passage of 2183 through North Fork W.Va. The booster is not the same as the simpling device, controlled by an angle valve in the cab. The booster feeds a comparatively small amount of high pressure steam into the "used" (low pressure) steam exhausted from the rear cylinders to the front. The boost in steam pressure increased drawbar horsepower on the uphill haul and could be sustained over a long grade, unlike simpling. Lead added to the frame provided needed traction for the added power.

Bottom: If the exhaust from 2183 looks like it's being thrown up at a slightly forward angle, it is. To make room for front end throttle, the exhaust stand, petticoat pipe, and stack are set to throw the exhaust 5 degrees forward off the vertical. Engineer Scott has left his seat box to find a lump of coal to weigh down a message for the photographers. Coal supply in tender has disappeared from sight, even though the Mallet took on a full supply at Farm, about 15 miles back.

28 Pocahontas Land Forms

Gary E. Huddleston

Engineer Scott on Y-6b 2183 has just turned on "booster" (controlled by a globe valve) as head end passes Eckman on "Elkhorn Mountain." During electrification, Eckman was an engine terminal, and evidence of that terminal can be seen in the spur tracks at left.

B. F. Cutler

In former electrified territory (until 1950) near Kimball, W.Va., the *Powhatan Arrow* drifts west out of twin tunnel that extra 2183, eight years later, would be heading upgrade through. (See photo of 2183 page 26)

Gary E. Huddleston

Top Left: Blowers at Elkhorn Tunnel are about to go on as 2199, assisted by three Alco road switchers on the rear, nears the top of the Appalachian Plateau in June 1959. The 7,107 ft. bore derives its name from Elkhorn Creek, which the train has been ascending since Welch. (Maximum grade is 1.4%.) The old tunnel, which this one replaced, is about a half-mile away; its single track and narrow clearances made for pure hell for the crews until the line was electrified. Slide detector fence, showing over top of coal cars, protects against slides from weathering sandstones and shales.

E. L. Huddleston

Below: The brick depot in the small town of Narrows, Va., has a lovely setting on the middle New River between two great parallel ridges, trending southwest to northeast. The actual "narrows" in the river is behind the photographer about two miles where the New cuts through the backbone of the ridge forming East River Mountain and Peters Mountain. The high ridge rising in the background above the town is aptly named Angel's Rest, altitude 3,633 ft. above sea level. The NS train is eastbound, April 1986.

Norfolk and Western Photo/John A. Rehor Collection

Bottom Left:At Bluefield, W.Va the edge of the Allegheny Front almost collides with the Ridge and Valley Province. Behind photographer (facing the passenger station) is the ridge of East River Mountain (which forms the state line) and on other side of the shallow valley is the tumbled landscape of the Plateau. This undated photo of two, two-unit straight electric locomotives bringing an eastbound coal train into the yard was before 1950, when electrification ended. Strung out along the narrow valley is the yards where crews were changed. West of Bluefield was electrified. East of Bluefield, the railroad descended to the level of the New River, which which both N&W and Virginian followed upstream into the Ridge and Valley Province. "Steam" emitted from vapor vents on the electric locomotives is from cooling of liquid rheostat.

Pocahontas Land Forms **31**

"I'd been asking about these cliffs, known as the Eggleston Palisades, and as we paddled [our canoe] around a bend on the river Shawn said, "There they are." The palisades are crumbling browns and grays . . . on river right, rising almost straight up and as high as four hundred feet."

– from Noah Adams
(National Public Radio commentator),
*Far Appalachia:
Following the New River North*
(Delacorte, 2001).

H. Reid
An N&W 2-8-8-2 Mallet, heading west down the New River near Pembroke, Va., is dwarfed by the huge cliffs of dolomite (sedimentary rock akin to limestone) that line the palisades of the New in this area. The train will soon enter 299 ft. Pembroke Tunnel, double tracked. Photographer H. Reid was standing behind the paralleling tracks of the Virginian, which became part of the N&W in 1959.

John Krause, T. W. Dixon, Jr. collection

N&W 2163 (2-8-82) crosses the Blue Ridge, on its way from Crewe to Roanoke, taking a long train of empty coal cars back to the mines in 1954. Nothing in the landscape pictured gives a clue that the locale is the Blue Ridge Mountains of Virginia—neither rock structure nor shape of the hill in background. There's not room for seeing the larger scene, of surrounding mountains like the Twin Peaks of Otter. Only one clue suggests the 1.35% ascent to get to Buford Gap at Blue Ridge station. And that clue is the skyrocketing exhaust!

N&W; Roanoke Chapter NRHS

Top Left: Mallet no. 2141 heads up New River west (north) of Pembroke around 1940. The train has stopped for the photographer in a remote location. The river, in cutting across the Ridge and Valley Province, has entrenched itself some 400 ft. below the "Valley" level into a thick bed of dolomite that because of vertical fractures, weathers into vertical columns, or spires.

N&W; VPI&SU Archives

Bottom Left: N&W coal train along the New River is moving south (east) beyond the bed of dolomite marking the Palisades and has passed through the Ridge and Valley Province, with Big Walker Mountain in the distance, the easternmost major ridge in the Province. The Virginian main line (now NS) is on east side of the river.

E. L. Huddleston

Both: J. Parker Lamb

Top Left: Descending from the summit of Flattop Mountain, at Glen Lyn, on the W.Va. and Virginia border, three EL-Cs brake their loaded coal train safely across the famous New River bridge (only the piers stand now) in 1960, right after the merger and before a connection had been built on the paralleling lines. N&W double tracked main is at left. Straight to the left from highway bridge in distance is where N&W curves away from river and starts up steep grade along East River to Bluefield.

Bottom Left: Westbound N&W manifest (former Virginian) in June 1961 starts climb up to top of the Allegheny Front at the spectacular bridge over the New (and over the N&W main) at Glen Lyn, Va. (at the W.Va. border).

Two powerful ignitron-rectifier "motors" wait at Elmore Yards along the upper Guyandotte River to shove a drag to the top of the Allegheny Plateau, where from east of Princeton the lead locomotives will use regenerative braking down the slope of the Allegheny Front to Glen Lyn and beyond. These EL-Cs, each rated at 3,300 H.P., were less than one year old in the fall of 1957. Seam of coal visible in the cut above the locomotive illustrates how rocks in the uplifted plateau are horizontal in bedding.

J. Parker Lamb

Three years later the electrics are gone and 3 N&W Geeps and one Alco RS-11 road switcher (second unit) cross the New at Glen Lyn, having left Elmore yard some three hours earlier. By the time this train gets to end of this bridge, it will almost be at the valley floor. It will then proceed up the New on the opposite bank from the N&W's Roanoke-Bluefield line.

E. L. Huddleston

In April 1986, a westbound NS manifest, downgrade on the New River; will soon cross river on a new bridge. Scene is near Pembroke on former Virginian electrified trackage. Across river are dolomite bluffs by-passed by N&W's 299-ft. Pembroke Tunnel. (pages 32-33)

E. L. Huddleston

Before the old Virginian reached Roanoke, it had left the New River, climbed the divide into the Great Valley via a tunnel, and headed east along the Roanoke River, at right. In 1948, westbound manifest leaves for Elmore on a winter afternoon, as a Mike switches in background.

C. W. Jernstrom

Westbound Virginian class AG 2-6-6-6 articulated brings empties (with stone on head end) through the Virginia Piedmont at Altavista,in 1947. Connecting tracks lead to the Southern main line, which crosses Virginian on overhead bridge. Within a little more than ten miles, train will start up 0.6% grade of Goose Creek.

Everett N. Young

Discolored CRR F7 leaves the Breaks at Pool Point bridge, in Kentucky, heading north to C&O connection at Elkhorn City, with manifest no. 95, numbered the same on both roads (at this time, February 1971). Sheer rock walls on both sides of Russell Fork of the Big Sandy, plus distance down to stream, made for a bridge that looked like it belonged in the Rockies more than in Appalachia.

Everett N. Young

Looking other direction as CRR F7 and an FP7 (with steam generator) work upgrade southbound out of Pool Point Tunnel with a 1977 excursion returning to Kingsport, Tenn.

B. F. Cutler

A little less than a mile south of Pool Point Tunnel is 1,523 ft. State Line Tunnel in the gorge of the Breaks, where in 1952 CRR management arranged for photographer to get to this spot by rail. The summit of Pine Mountain, above the tunnel, marks the Ky.-Va. state line. F7s are southbound, up 1.35% grade, reduced to 1.2% in tunnel.

Everett N. Young

Emerging from 7,854 ft. Sandy Ridge Tunnel, CRR SD40 3011 (leading 3 units) heads north with manifest no 95 past coal mine at Trammel, Va. in 1974. South of here the coal measures of the Appalachian Plateau quickly play out, for beyond Dante, on the south side of the tunnel, the CRR tracks drop down into the valley of the Clinch River, in Ridge and Valley Province.

**M. B. Connery,
C. K. Marsh collection**

Besides the Breaks and the Loops, a traveler over the Clinchfield would find a third remarkable piece of scenery—the Nolichucky River gorge, by which the railroad leaves the Great Valley and climbs the Blue Ridge to an elevation of 2,628 ft. at the summit Loops. (That is almost exactly the same elevation of the N&W mainline at Bluefield, WVa.) Three and a half miles into the Gorge photographer leans out cab of engine 3608 on southbound freight in 1975. Complex and very hard rocks of the Blue Ridge make for such steep sides that concrete shoring is needed to provide space for road bed.

B. F. Cutler, H. H. Harwood coll.
Skaggs Hole Bridge and Skaggs Tunnel are about 4 and a half miles south from Pool Point on Russell Fork. Train is headed north. Horizontal bedding of rocks indicate Pine Mountain anticline has been passed.

Everett N. Young
CRR Extra 3019 south (SD40) leads 200, 3024, and 909 out of 752 ft. Sykes Mill Tunnel near Clinchco, Va., in 1976. This is one of 20 tunnels the Clinchfield encountered in the first 33 miles south of Elkhorn City through the rugged Appalachian Plateau, culminating with the longest on the road—Sandy Ridge Tunnel at the Cumberland Front.

The CRR follows the Clinch River for about 40 miles, in pretty much a straight compass line to the southwest, before tunneling under Clinch Mountain, second longest on the road. Nevertheless, the River has lots of meanders, which the railroad must negotiate. Near Bangor, Va., extra 200 north has stopped with an excursion at the confluence of the Guest River with the Clinch off the left edge of the picture.

Railroad bridges, like this one across the Nolichucky River at Chestoa, Tenn. usually produce "S" curves because they are built at right angles to the stream. Twenty-three phosphate loads from Florida are on the head end of northbound no. 93 and empty coal cars extend around curve beyond bridge, where the 9-mile gorge begins.

High up in the Blue Ridge, but still following a water level grade (the North Toe River) a northbound freight in 1947 drifts downgrade past lumber yard at Spruce Pine, North Carolina. Though class L-3 2-8-8-2 no. 740 is built to the same major dimensions as the USRA 2-8-8-2s of 1919, 740 does not look like a USRA Mallet. Bigger cab, bigger stack and higher sand and steam domes throw off one's expectations.

Left: Having descended the southeastern slope of the Blue Ridge (in distance) via the Loops, F7 no. 803, southbound, crosses the 921 ft. Catawba River bridge, built 1908, at Lake James in the Piedmont Province just north of Marion, in 1951.

Earl M. Walker, C. K. Marsh, Jr. collection
About 25 miles upstream from Chestoa, approaching Toecane, North Carolina, a southbound coal train climbs toward Blue Ridge summit along the Toe River, continuation of the Nolichucky. Challenger type, 4-6-6-4, pushes. Jumbled Blue Ridge summits, nearly 5,000 ft. in elevation, show in background, forming state line with Tennessee.

Fireman hollered: "Casey, you're going too fast,
You run the block-board the last station we passed."
Casey says: "Yes, but I think we'll make it through,
For she's steaming better than ever I knew."

– Ballad of Casey Jones

Speed records were possible in the flatlands of central Mississippi. They were not possible in the Appalachians, no matter how well engineered the tracks. In fact, the Illinois Central main line near Vaughan, Mississippi, on which Casey Jones plowed into the rear of a parked train, was one where passenger train speed records were typically made. According to figures in Donald M. Steffee's Annual Speed Survey for 1948 (*Railroad*, April 1949) between Canton and Jackson, Mississippi, territory just south of Vaughan, the diesel powered *Panama Limited* was scheduled to run 73.6 mph. Because the train stopped at both stations, speeds of ninety or better would have to be made to keep to the schedule.

The old gospel hymn "Life's Railway to Heaven" invokes the warning, "Watch the curves, the fills, the trestles" (and slides, it might have added). These were problem areas of construction that occur with greater frequency as terrain gets more mountainous. Running downhill is also associated with wrecks, both in history and folk songs, like "The Wreck of the Old 97." One knows for a fact that as land forms increase in elevation the railroads built through them require longer to run through. Steffee's Annual Speed Survey bears this out. Of course, in the case of the Virginian and the Clinchfield, neither road served large enough population centers to warrant more than local service. Author Peter Maiken does point out in his *Night Trains* that the Virginian once had Pullman service between Norfolk and Roanoke but it was canceled early in the Depression. Only C&O and N&W served population centers large enough and spaced from each other far enough to warrant named trains running all night. (complicating this assessment is N&W's instituting an all daylight streamliner, *The Powhatan Arrow*, right after World War II.)

Thus C&O and N&W are represented in Steffee's 1948 Survey, which covers start-to-stop runs of 60 mph and over for diesel and steam powered trains. At that time both roads were steam. However, C&O had a year earlier absorbed the Pere Marquette, with lines mostly in Michigan. Its diesel powered eastbound *Pere Marquette* made 63.9 mph over the mostly glaciated outwash plains between Lansing and Plymouth. (The westbound version had a fairly long

.90% grade out of Plymouth to slow it down slightly.) On the "old' C&O and on the N&W (before its mergers) speeds over 60 all occurred on sections of the mainline west of the Appalachian Plateau and east of the Blue Ridge (and Piedmont). The N&W crossed the Atlantic Coastal Plain over long tangents and on mostly level track. It was across the Tidewater section of Virginia, between Petersburg and Suffolk, that the *Powhatan Arrow* westbound made start-to-stop 63.1 mph and eastbound 62.0 mph. The area for speed over the old C&O is perhaps a little harder to comprehend, for C&O's fastest speeds, mostly with the *George Washington* (in two sections). were in the Ohio Valley east of the Cincinnati metropolitan area. If one looks at a relief map he sees the Ohio River's fairly narrow valley is set between high hills all the way east, thus earning it the name "beautiful Ohio." The top of the hills is actually the top of plateaus. The "Cincinnati arch" accounts for the high hills just to the east of Cincinnati, and beyond the arch (with no clear demarcation other than some "knobs") is the Appalachian Plateau all the way to Pittsburgh. Yet the flood plain of the valley is level for railroad purposes and the river, still in a "cutting" process, has no oxbow curves requiring sharp bends of the roadbed laid down its flood plain. On top of that is the superior engineering, which under the direction of Chief Engineer Harry Frazier, kept the tracks free of "dips" and the curves to less than two degrees. (The longest tangent on this line is six miles west of Greenup, Ky.)

The Cincinnati Division thus became the C&O's race track. The *George Washington*, in both directions between South Portsmouth, Ky., and Maysville, Ky., was carded at 62.7 mph, 0.40 mph less than the N&W's *Powhatan Arrow* across the Tidewater flats of the Virginia shore. Between Newport (suburb of Cincinnati) to Augusta and Vanceburg to South Portsmouth, all small towns on the "CD," the *George Washington* (both Washington and Richmond sections) and the *Sportsman* had scheduled start to stop speeds ranging from 60.3 mph to 61.6 mph. To maintain these schedules required over-the-road speeds of between eighty and ninety. In 1946 C&O formally tested a Pennsylvania Railroad class T-1 4-4-4-4 Duplex steam passenger locomotive on its named

J. R. Quinn

Powhatan Arrow leaves Kenova station (top left background) July 2, 1947. No. 607, easily capable of 90 mph, will average only 42 mph for the 73 miles to Williamson. which lists no stops for the one hour, 45 minute run. Why so slow for N&W's premier train? First, are the curves necessary to keep the railroad following the flood plain of the Tug Fork. Second, is the stop at Prichard (unlisted) to take coal. This writer, who rode the *Arrow* from Ironton to Williamson in 1953, recalls that at the Prichard coal dock the class J stayed coupled to its train while making 3 separate spottings under the chute to level the supply.

E. L. Huddleston
At East Portsmouth engine terminal in December 1958, a 2-8-8-2 clears its cylinders of accumulated moisture as it prepares to go to work. Class J 601 is on stand-by. Access from cab to cat walk, stoker engine under cab, and extra generator over second driver are details showing up on this streamlined gem.

passenger trains system wide. Maximum speed on all tests for the T-1 was 82.5 mph, attained between Vanceburg, Ky., and Maysville, Ky. on the "C.D."

By 1948 the engines pulling the heavy-weight Pullman trains over the C.D. were the world's heaviest Hudsons, class L-2, which had essentially the same sized boiler and firebox as the C&O (and NKP, PM, and VGN) 2-8-4 freight engines, having been both designed by the Advisory Mechanical Committee. (But of course, they had much larger driving wheels and shorter piston stroke to make them go faster.) With the large firebox and boiler and high drivers, the C&O class L-2 4-6-4s were capable of moving "a 15-car passenger train at 90 miles an hour on straight level track," according to historian Walter A. Lucas. In 1948, because the last order of L-2s were not received until mid-summer, there were five rebuilt F-19 class Pacifics still pulling named trains on the C.D. These five 4-6-2s had been rebuilt to 4-6-4s in C&O's Huntington Shops in 1946 and 1947 to power the Louisville and Richmond-Newport News sections of the projected daylight streamliner, *The Chessie*, which on the mainline runs would have been powered by 3 steam-turbo-electric locomotives built by Baldwin-Westinghouse in 1947. Nos. 490-494 were given a new classification—L-1—even though they were rebuilt to Hudsons after class L-2 nos. 300-307 had been received new from Baldwin Locomotive Works. A curve elimination project was undertaken in the Alleghenies that supposedly would have enabled the stillborn *Chessie* to maintain a twelve-hour schedule between Cincinnati and Washington.

According to research by Jessie J. Smith, the *Chessie's* real purpose was not to supplement C&O's existing through passenger service but to ferry well heeled patrons to the famed Greenbrier in White Sulphur Springs, serving much like a five-star hotel's limousine. That would explain the train's lavish appointments, as cataloged by Smith: "An on-board movie theater showing the latest Hollywood films. Sure! ... And a children's nurse in the Family Coach to help change diapers and prepare formulae? Of course! ...And a children's playroom, coloring books with crayons and a tiny Disney cartoon movie theater? ...The *Chessie's* amenities were just

E. L. Huddleston

Passenger traffic is so good that C&O has put on an extra section of the Cincinnati-Washington *F.F.V.* for New Years Day 1948. It's about 3 in the afternoon at Ashland, Ky. The advanced (coach) section at right is powered by a Hudson (L-1) rebuilt from a heavy Pacific, and the main section (Pullman) by Hudson 306 (L-2), built in 1942 as world's heaviest, Light Pacific (F-15) at left will take local to Elkhorn City.

N&W wisely adopted system-wide use of its 4-8-4s in mainline passenger service, which cut down costs of servicing and duplications of power. C&O, more traditional, had, since introducing the Mountain type in 1911, used Pacifics or Hudsons on the level divisions and Mountains or Greenbriers on the mountain. Here at Hinton, Hudson 303 has come from Huntington or Cincinnati with mail-express train 104. Greenbrier 610 will take over for the Alleghany and Mountain Subdivisions to Charlottesville. Unused coaling station for *Chessie* stream-liner is at left.

normal services for the 'resort crowd.' The train's on-board library, original oil paintings, and the industrial exhibits throughout the train weren't there for the common passenger boarding at Mineral or Mt. Carbon. ...The dome cars, ceiling-height aquarium, and soda fountains were not available for residents of Goshen or Gauley."

When the *Chessie* was never put in service, these five fine steam passenger locomotives were available for use. It is said that everything was new on these engines except the boiler and firebox! The class F-19 that they had been rebuilt from were recognized as an exceptionally fine model of the late 1920s, built right before the Super Power revolution. But now, rebuilt from 4-6-2s into 4-6-4s, they were Super Power and they had the latest "valve gear"—poppet valves operated with tappets like auto engine valves.

Luckily, a C&O locomotive engineer who ran these engines on the Cincinnati Division recorded for posterity what it was like to speed along the C.D. with an L-1, throttle wide open. In 1983 Stuart Leuthner published the "voice histories" of retired railroaders into a book titled *The Railroaders*. Among those interviewed was former C.D. engineer Homer D. Lewis. He recalled, "It might have been engine 491 or 492, I'm not sure which, that I had on a run [train no. 6, the *F.F.V.*] between [South] Portsmouth and Russell. I felt that engine trembling, just trembling like a little fox

terrier. To myself I said, What's the matter? I looked up at the speedometer and it was sitting on ninety-two miles per hour." The trembling was of course the "dynamic augment" produced by the force of the main and side rods on the drive wheels, making them jump "up and down," even though the weights of the rods were balanced by counterweights added to the drivers. Mr. Lewis does not mention his fireman, but to get an engine running that fast would require making plenty of steam. Even though the L-1 had a modern mechanical stoker, operated by its own small steam engine, it still took skill in knowing when to feed coal and to what portions of the firebox to send the coal to. (Steam jets propelled the coal to all or portions of the big firebox.)

Even more than good firing was the fact that the five rebuilt Hudsons had been equipped with the "Franklin system of steam distribution," otherwise known as poppet valves. The piston valve, which poppet valves replaced, had a major disadvantage: it joined the steam intake and exhaust functions in the same stroke, and it opened and closed with such relative slowness that the steam could not be exhausted completely before the main piston began its power stoke, a condition producing "back pressure" against the power stroke. The higher the speed, the higher the back pressure. Poppet valves, similar in design to automotive valves, separated and speeded up the

In June 1948, in process of delivery, no. 612, part of order for 5 J-3 passenger engines for mountain territory service, prepares for break-in run east to Hinton at Ashland, Ky., 34th St. yards. In principal dimensions. 610-614 was identical with the earlier J-3s with one important exception. On the 1948 order the combustion chamber ahead of the smokebox was made a foot longer, reducing the tubes and flues to 20 ft. in length, ideal for best absorption of heat. And increasing size of combustion chamber allowed for a better "combination of combustibles and air." (Ralph Johnson).

intake and exhaust functions; instead of a single valve, there were eight for each cylinder (for type A two intake and two exhaust valves on each end of the cylinder, six inches in diameter.) Because poppet valves increased the steam passage area both inward and outward, they reduced back pressure, always a problem in high-speed short cut-off passenger service. Reducing back pressure materially increased cylinder horsepower.

Few other steam locomotives in America had been equipped with these valves. They came a little late to be adopted wide scale. But C&O wanted a 'state of the art" passenger locomotive, and thus substituted poppet valves for the customary sliding thimble type valve. Franklin Railway Supply had improved considerably the original system invented by the Italian Caprotti. The Franklin type A valve was first developed, followed by type B. The 1948 order of L-2 Hudsons to supplement 300-307 had type B. L-1 class 490-494 had the type A. In principle, the Franklin type A valves on the L-1 and the type B on the L-2s of 1948 worked the same. Both types employed separately controlled intake and exhaust valves, similar to those in auto engines, rather than 14-inch diameter piston valve–the size used on class L-2 nos. 300-307 with so-called Baker valve gear. Type A employed oscillating cams for the tappets while the type B employed continuous-contour rotating cams. Also, the power transmission to drive the two types differed. In 1947, a Franklin ad stated, (1) "In the Type A System, the poppet valves are arranged on two levels–two intake and two exhaust valves for each end of each cylinder with the Type A and two intake and three exhaust valves with the type A-1." (2) "The Drive [of the type A] is taken from both locomotive crossheads and delivered to the valve-box located on the center-line of the locomotive. Here it is separated into the component motions required for intake and exhaust cam shafts

and is delivered to the right and left cam boxes. The cam boxes are located on the cylinders, between the steam chests. Intermediate levers, one for each valve, follow the cams, and actuate the valve tappets." The key, then, to the Type A system is the valve gear box, located out of sight in the center above the fame and just behind the cylinders. The action of the piston at the crosshead drives a link resembling the "combination lever" used with conventional valve gear. That link in turn drives other links connected to the gear box translating reciprocating motion into oscillating motion for actuating the cam shafts. The advantage of the Type B was the rotary cam shaft, simpler in operation and having fewer moving parts than the Type A. If the complexity of the Type A produced any problems on the class L-1 rebuilt Hudsons 490-494, they were not apparent to the casual observer, for the L-1s seemed to handle their trains always on schedule and without breaking down.

Much excellent research has been done on modern Norfolk and Western steam power; e. g., Ken Miller's *Norfolk and Western Class J: The Finest Steam Passenger Locomotive*. Unlike C&O, which used two groupings of passenger locomotives, one for the flatlands divisions and the other for mountain, the N&W used just one grouping, notably the class J 4-8-4 and the class K-2 4-8-2 system wide. (The class K-2 had originally been a design of the United States Railroad Administration assigned to the N&W in World War I. N&W liked them so well they bought ten copies in 1923. They were streamlined right after World War II.) In a pleasing coincidence, Leuthner's *The Railroaders* contains another railroader's account of passenger train running in the Ohio Valley in the Portsmouth area, only this fast running was done on the other side of the river from Homer D. Lewis's. The Norfolk and Western's main line runs parallel with the C&O's Cincinnati Division between

E. L. Huddleston

A year after it was scheduled to go in service on 12-hour run in daylight between Washington and Cincinnati, *Chessie* streamliner is displayed at Huntington, WV in 1948. No 502 was one of three steam-turbo-electric locomotives built especially for this completely new train, whose costs overran any possible return on investment. As Bill Withuhn wrote, World War II veterans did not want to ride trains; they had had enough as draftees of the government ferrying them around.

Portsmouth and Ironton in Ohio. (South Portsmouth, Ky. and Russell, Ky. are equivalent stations on the C&O side.) Flood plain topography is the same and the curves as gentle. Homer Lewis was piloting the *F.F.V.* George H. Kelch of the N&W was running the *Pocahontas.* Mr. Kelch, who became a locomotive inspector, recalls: "The fastest I ever run, it was one of them K-2s. I don't know if it was no. 126 or 127 [K-2a, Baldwin 1923]. I was firing on train No. 3 one morning between Portsmouth, Ohio, and Williamson, West Virginia. ...We were about an hour late when I told him [engineer Mark Pleasants]. 'Run the damn stoker and let me run the engine and we'll try to make up some of the time.' I run down through Haverhill [Ohio] and Sheelersburg [Wheelersburg, Ohio], and I'm telling you, that engine was right around eighty or ninety miles an hour. I commenced to ease it off, you never shut one clear off, and I was still running sixty-five miles an hour when we came down through the yard. [East Portsmouth]."

The fact that there was no "race track' on the N&W between Portsmouth and Cincinnati illustrates the effect of topography on fast running. As noted above, the C&O followed the flood plain of the Ohio River valley all the way down the "C.D." The N&W's was geographically more direct, but the route, back in the hills, followed the twists and turns of streams in the Appalachian Plateau for much of the way from Portsmouth to Cincinnati. Although this route through southern Ohio was a few miles shorter than the river route it was so crooked that its nickname was "The Peavine," a term used on other railroads, as well, to denote a piece of track where running was slower than it ought to be because of zig-zags and hills and dales.

Even though streamlining helped popularize a railroad's image, streamlining of steam passenger locomotives in mountain service was not very often done because it was hard to keep them clean if they ran through tunnels, which were common enough in mountain territory. And since streamlining implied the great speeds, and since steam locomotives in mountain service usually could not make great speeds, one usually associated "streamliners" with flatlands service, like the dash from Chicago to Milwaukee. That is, one thought this way until the Norfolk and Western took 4-8-4s, usually thought of a mountain territory engines, and streamlined them for use system wide. N&W ran its class K-2 4-8-2s and world famous class J 4-8-4s both through tunnel territory and over less mountainous divisions. Both had attractive, complete, and functional cowling decorating a conventional but very powerful passenger steam locomotive. The cowling was home-styled, by the chief passenger car foreman at the Roanoke Shops where the class Js were built. Its symmetrical "bullet" front that jutted out over the pilot looked more sophisticated than the usual conical design used to "stream style" the smoke box front.

The fad for streamlining nearly everything— including electric toasters—was a part of the growth of interest in commercial airliners in the mid-1930s. Some of the leading industrial designers of the time were put to work on futuristic designs, like the famous New York Central Hudsons of Henry Dreyfuss. Other railroads did the streamlining in their own shops, either because like the N&W they built from scratch their own locomotives or because they could not afford a designer. Some of the designs, esthetically, were quite successful, like the N&W class J 4-8-4 and its class K-2 4-8-2. Other designs looked like inverted bathtubs. C&O's homemade design on its five Pacifics rebuilt to class L-1 Hudsons were in between. The front end style of the C&O Hudsons imitated the front end of the steam-turbo-electrics, class M-1, nos. 500-502 that were intended to pull the mainline sections of the *Chessie*, a daylight streamliner between Washington and Cincinnati. C&O backed out of this ambitious project, even though the equipment and three steam-turbo-electric locomotives had already been delivered in 1947. Both B&O with its *Cincinnatian* and N&W with its *Powhatan Arrow* went ahead with their competing streamliners, both pulled by streamlined steam locomotives. Who at Baldwin, or within C&O's motive power department, designed the streamlining for the class M-1 turbines is unknown. As noted above, passenger car foreman Frank Noel, following management's instructions, designed a casing that preserved the look of power of the new Class J 4-8-4s of 1941 but that added proportional smoothness and harmony of lines. Larry Sagle, in *B&O Power*, disclosed that the four P-7d heavy Pacifics streamlined for service on the new *Cincinnatian*, were designed by Miss Olive Dennis, the first woman civil engineer on the B&O. Sagle added, "President Willard had been so impressed at finding a woman engineer on the staff that he assigned her to special duties."

Streamlining steam locomotives in the 1930s and 1940s became so widespread that, besides N&W, C&O, and B&O, there were at least twelve other major railroads in the United States (not counting Canada) that had streamlined passenger engines, usually Pacifics or Hudsons. Keeping them clean was important not only for the "polish" associated with cleanliness but because the streamlining usually involved bright colors in combination rather than the typically uniform black of unstreamlined steamers. Soot on the fronts of a black locomotive could be tolerated; it could not on a streamlined. That is one reason C&O ran its streamlined rebuilt Hudsons on level portions of the system. (Of course, C&O usually ran Mountain or Northern types on its mountain divisions anyway.) N&W ran its two streamlined classes—Mountains and Northerns—system wide on both level and mountain divisions. But N&W had a state of the art locomotive washer, pictured so dramatically on p. 55 of Miller's *Norfolk and Western Class J*. This device, installed in 1946 at Shaffers Crossing, Roanoke, was automatic. It clearly reminds one of the roller, brush, and spray assemblies encountered in upscale commercial car washes in present-day America.

When one thinks of passenger trains on the Pocahontas roads, he thinks of the scheduled named trains mostly, because railroads spent money and effort advertising them. But there were the locals, all with numbers, assigned regular crews and listed in public timetables, that ran to obscure places and made no money for the roads but which were provided for the convenience of coal operators and coal and railroad company employees before good roads came to the mountains. Often the locals enabled mountain youth to attend high school, as Dale Ernest was able to do riding a C&O local daily from Thurmond up Loup

Creek to Mt. Hope and back. The engine on his train was a Consolidation (2-8-0), usually thought of as a freight engine. But on steep mountain grades you didn't need high-drivered locomotives. That is why it is hard to understand how C&O ended up with Ten-Wheelers (4-6-0) with 73-inch drivers. Even the famous Pennsylvania Class G-5s Ten Wheeler of the early 1920s–so efficient with commuter trains—had only 68-inch drivers. For comparison's sake, it is well to keep in mind that the steam locomotive possessing the highest drivers of any C&O locomotive—78 inches—was the class L-2 Hudson (4-6-4) of 1942-1948, which could take 16 cars 90 mph on level track. Turn-of-the-century C&O class F-11, which had 62-inch drivers, was working as a branch-line freight engine in the late 1940s. (No. 377 of this class is on display at the B&O Museum in Baltimore.) Classes F-12 and F-13, nos. 86-92, with their 73-inch drivers and high-mounted boilers, were about the best proportioned of C&O's smaller passenger locomotives. Built 1910 to 1913, these Ten Wheelers came to C&O via the Hocking Valley merger. The HV, which ran mostly over level or low-grade trackage from Athens to Toledo in Ohio, could use high-stepping steeds like these.

Passenger trains were not limited to scheduled trains Whether in the mountains or over more level divisions there were special movements. Funeral trains for dignitaries come first to mind, like Franklin Roosevelt's mournful return from Georgia to Washington, then circus trains, then excursions to state fairs and to sporting events. Illustrating the importance of excursions to railroad passenger service is an item in *Railway Review* for July 1919 taking to task the United States Railroad Administration, which still controlled the railroads, for "failure to install popular priced excursions to various seaside and summer resorts." (The magazine claimed that, World War I being over, it was time "to encourage travel.")

Tour buses today have largely taken the place of excursion trains. But there are still special trains run on passenger train schedules for Presidents or candidates for President. And the Ringling Brothers Barnum Bailey circus still travels by train—a very long train, it might be added. A special is still run in Kentucky to the Kentucky Derby in May, but excursions to race tracks, in whatever form, have been largely replaced by buses to gambling casinos. Most excursions were run in areas of dense population; thus in Appalachia, unless there was a spa like Hot Springs, Va., or White Sulphur Springs, W.Va. , excursions were limited to festivals held at picturesque mountain locations or trips to scenic, historical, or commemorative sites. In later years, of course, railfan societies chartered excursions to operationally important points in Appalachia. There were excursions to Cincinnati Reds baseball games run on Sundays (Crosley Field was in easy walking distance of Cincinnati Union Station.) And there were specials to other sporting events. This writer remembers being in Huntington, W.Va. in the fall of 1947 on a Saturday, and there at the C&O station was an F-17 Pacific ready to depart with a special carrying fans to Charleston, for that afternoon Huntington East High School was scheduled to play Charleston Stonewall Jackson. (One wonders if the train crossed the old bridge over the Kanawha right into Charleston, running over NYC tracks.)

The special movement in Appalachia that has gained national media attention is the Santa Claus train, inaugurated in 1943 by businessmen in Kingsport, Tennessee, who wanted to express appreciation to the mountain folk of southwestern Virginia for supporting merchants in Kingsport and who wanted to spread cheer in the coal fields north of Kingsport. Riding on the observation platform of the CRR's *Blue Ridge*, Santa would dispense tons of goodies to children and adults who lined the tracks as the trained headed south first through the scenic Breaks and then into the rugged hills north of Dante and finally into the Valley and Ridge Province of northeastern Tennessee. True, the Cumberland Plateau had some big coal mines, such as at Moss or Trammel in Virginia, but it also had poverty. That poverty was widespread in the southern Appalachian coal fields even in the post- World War II boom years became clear to this writer in recalling his Dad going on runs as a freight brakeman up the "Guyan Valley" in West Virginia and taking with him on these runs candy and other treats for children who obviously were living in near hovels but who were waving at him as he stood on the caboose platform while his long train of coal cars wound up or down the Valley in serving the great Logan County coal fields.

It is this spirit of generosity and appreciation that captivated the nation's press. Captivating railfans are the locomotives that have hauled the train from the CRR's northern terminus at Elkhorn City to Kingsport., the most notable the little Ten-Wheeler No. 1, operated under steam, and the huge Union Pacific 4-6-6-4 Challenger type no. 3985, which came all the way from Wyoming to head up the train disguised as a Clinchfield Challenger. As Everett Young wrote, "This would be the first time [1991] since her birth in the halls of Alco's Schenectady Works that the engine [UP 3985] would be east of the Mississippi." Since it would not be appropriate to have a "foreign" 4-6-6-4 articulated locomotive running on a road that had owned its own 4-6-6-4s, UP no. 3985 was taken to CSX's Huntington locomotive shops and given appropriate lettering and numbering in order to resemble Clinchfield no. 676. (Oddly, numbering of the CRR's actual 4-6-6-4s ended with 675, although that was not the newest CRR Challenger.) No. 676 ran under its own steam on this one "Santa Claus" trip to Kingsport, before returning West, where its number was changed back to 3985.

Black Mountain Railroad's no. 1 was a very small Ten-Wheeler but it had a long history of service. Built in 1882 at Logansport, Indiana, for a predecessor of the "Panhandle" (which in turn became part of giant Pennsylvania), this 4-6-0 was sold in 1900 to a predecessor of the Clinchfield, the Ohio River and Charleston Ry., headquartered in Johnson City, Tennessee. It then went to the South and Western, which of course was the "mystery" name for the Carolina, Clinchfield, and Ohio, then under construction. As an odd-lot piece of motive power, it was sold in 1913 to the 10-mile long Black Mountain Ry. in the North Carolina Blue Ridge. In 1955, the Clinchfield (which owned the Black Mountain) donated No. 1 to the city of Erwin, which put it on display several years later. In 1968 the CRR decided to rebuild No. 1 and restore it for excursion service. From 1968 through 1978 (when it suffered frame failure), No. 1 hauled the Santa Claus special on its yearly run from Elkhorn city to Kingsport. Being something of a "lightweight" even as a Ten-Wheeler, No. 1 was assisted on the runs first by a single diesel with steam heat generator and later by two. As of the year 2000, the Santa Claus train attacked more attention than ever, with CNN giving its run full coverage. As for Black Mountain no. 1, in 1981, it was donated to the B&O Museum in Baltimore for display.

Passenger service on the four southern Appalachian, or "Pocahontas," roads ranged in steam days from informal mixed trains like N&W's "Huckleberry," to long Pullman trains on strictly maintained schedules. Diesels came to the C&O and N&W at about the time they sought permission to abandon money losing locals and mixed trains (peddler freights that handled both freight cars and paying passengers). So most of these trains never underwent the transition from steam power to diesel. however, C&O and N&W had through passenger trains that kept running until the inauguration of Amtrak at the end of April 1971. N&W used General Motors General Purpose locomotives, the famed 1750 H. P. "Geeps" right up to the end. They had taken over from the streamlined 4-8-4s. Geeps were not streamlined but had a well proportioned symmetry of line. And the Tuscan red color

Baltimore and Ohio, learning of C&O's much publicized intention to place in service a postwar streamliner between the Washington-Baltimore area and Cincinnati, preempted C&O's *Chessie* with the *Cincinnatian*, pictured at Athens, Ohio in 1947. Streamlining for this B&O heavy Pacific was different from streamlining of Pacific for Royal Blue earlier. C&O local at left will run over the old Hocking Valley line to Columbus. The heavy Pacific on this train is not normal, for an ex-HV Ten Wheeler usually powered it. This photo is to be treasured, for today there are no railroad tracks whatsoever within the city of Athens!

that N&W used on these Geeps—two in multiple on most trains—gave them a dignified appeal. (Geeps for freight service and Geeps for passenger differed mainly in the passenger units having an oil-fired steam generator—for passenger car heating—mounted in the section of the hood immediately ahead of the cab. (Or, on N&W Geeps, which were run "backwards," behind the cab.)

C&O had absorbed in 1947 the Pere Marquette, mainly a Michigan road very close to General Motors. So it followed PM's lead and ordered Geeps for freight service and for passenger service the model "E," intended only for passenger trains. PM had inaugurated its speedy *Pere Marquette* passenger trains between Chicago and Grand Rapids and on to Detroit using brand new General Motors model E7 diesels,

Pocahontas Passenger **57**

which were of course streamlined. When C&O dieselized its passenger trains early in 1952 it bought 30 model E8s (which had been introduced in 1949) for its mainline "named" trains. These, like the E7s, had two V-12 diesel engines in each unit. However, the E8s developed 2250 H.P. each and were usually operated in two or three unit multiples on each train, depending on length. These locomotives had the ability to accelerate a "heavy" passenger train from a station stop with smoothness and with a speed build-up that made riding behind the units a pleasure. Each C&O E8 was 70 ft., four inches long, and was pow-ered by two, two-cycle V-12 engines. Instructions were issued not to run them above 80 mph, although they were geared for 92. While they attained that speed on the "race track" Cincinnati Division, they did not on the New River mainline, which had a timetable maximum speed of 60 mph from Hinton to just east of Quinnimont, and 50 mph from Quinnimont to Kanawha Falls.

The very last word on Pocahontas region passenger trains belongs to Louis D. Rubin, Jr., distinguished author of *A Memory of Trains* (USC Press, 2000): "What I remember most vividly of all about [Robert

George Washington and the Appalachian Crossing

After the War for independence, George Washington, wanting to keep the West away from the influence of the British and sensing the potential for the future growth of America, started looking for paths across the Appalachians connecting his native Virginia with the interior—specifically the Ohio Valley and the Great Lakes territory.

While encamped at Newburgh, New York, in 1783 (the year of the peace treaty with Britain), Washington had traveled up the Mohawk and was delighted to discover how easily developed would be this "water level" route to Lake Erie and the West. But it was his native Virginia that he was most interested in seeing developed commercially, so almost as soon as he was freed of military duties he made a trip to discover the best possible canal and portage routes over the Appalachians. On his 1784 trip he interviewed frontiersmen in the Great Valley and elsewhere who knew what lay beyond the summits of the Appalachians. (Washington had planned to go past the frontier himself but Indian uprisings made a trans-Appalachian journey impractical.) He discovered there were three useful routes: up the Potomac and across the divide to the Little Youghiogheny; from the James and Jackson up Dunlap Creek and thence to Howards Creek, the Greenbrier, New, and Kanawha to the Ohio; and up the Roanoke river from the Great Valley over the Atlantic-Gulf divide to the New, and on to the Holston or to the Kanawha.

Washington was not impressed with the Roanoke route, for even though there was only a fairly low divide between this river and the New and even though this route intersected Daniel Boone's Wilderness Trail in the Great Valley, the Roanoke flowed out of Virginia into the state of North Carolina. (The Virginian and the N&W of course utilized the low divide between the Roanoke and the New, tunneling under it.) The James and the Potomac were the rivers a native Virginian should consider. Washington made this clear in a letter to John Filson, Kentucky writer and explorer, on January 15, 1785: "That the river Potomac communicates by short portages...with the Yohoghaney [sic] and Cheat Rivers...for the countries East and West of the Appalachian mountains, as James River also does with the Waters of the Great Kanwha [sic], none can deny, and that these will be the channels thro' which the trade of the Western country will principally come, I have no more doubt of myself, than the states of Virginia and Maryland had, when within these few days, they have passed laws for the purpose of extending and improving the navigation of these rivers, and opening roads of communication between them and the Western waters."

While both the Potomac and James routes were important to the state of Virginia, the James-Kanawha route was more truly Virginian than the Potomac-Youghiogheny because Richmond, principal city and capital, was on the James. Alexandria was the only town of significance on the Potomac, which at that time had as much importance to Marylanders as to Virginians. Some 40 years later, Claudius Crozet, Principal Engineer for the Virginia Board of Public Works, surveyed canal and railroad routes to the west for the state. He reported that there were two equally feasible rail routes: "...from the head of the valley of... James River, or of Roanoke, there is only one ridge to be passed over, after which , the Valley of New River may be pursued down to the Ohio." Crozet proved prescient, for almost half a century later, the Chesapeake and Ohio appropriated essentially the same James-to-New River route; the Norfolk and Western came to the New by way of the Roanoke, but left the New before its confluence with the Great Kanawha in order to tap the coal field later named the Pocahontas. (Before discovery of the Pocahontas seams, the N&W did intend to go down the New.)

E. L. Huddleston

C&O Hudson no. 491 leaves Ashland. Ky., in 1948 with the *F.F.V.* on 309 mile run from Hinton to Cincinnati. 491 was one of five F-19 Pacifics rebuilt in 1946-47 for use on side sections of the main *Chessie* train; that is, from Ashland to Louisville and Charlottesville to Newport News-Norfolk. When *Chessie* was canceled, the 5 Hudsons were put into regular level-land mainline passenger pool. James K. Millard stated the stainless steel arch rising from the headlight "imparted a certain Greco-Roman look to the front end." This writer, a supporter of the Michigan State Spartans, can be more specific. the arch looks like the ridge on a Spartan warrior's helmet that extends forward as a nose guard.

R.] Young's valiant effort to make the C&O's passenger service more attractive to the riding public was something that took place on a cold early Sunday morning in late winter, not long after I had first come to Staunton [to work as newspaper city editor in 1947]. I had checked the first copy of the paper to come off the press, stopped at the all-night restaurant for supper, then gone back to my room. I read awhile, then tried to go to sleep, but I was unable to do so. It was getting on toward daybreak, and I decided to dress, go over to the station, and take the *George Washington* home to Richmond. The night air was penetratingly cold, and there was snow everywhere. Tired, shivering, I waited for the train to arrive from the west. At length the double-headed 2-8-4's [among many C&O Kanawhas equipped for passenger ser-

vice] came into the station at the head of the long train, and I went aboard a coach. I placed my suitcase on a seat and walked back to wait for the dining car's scheduled opening. Others were already in line. I was still chilled from my vigil on the train platform. Not long after the *George Washington* left Staunton the doors to the double-coach dining car opened. Before the waiters began taking orders they walked along the tables and poured out steaming demitasse cups of thick black railroad coffee for all present. Sipping it, watching through the fogged windows as the train moved across the snowy Blue Ridge, I was very grateful. It was a small thing, a creature comfort I have never forgotten."

Rail Photo Service, E. L. Huddleston collection

Streamlining altered the appearance of a steam locomotive radically as revealed in comparison of streamlined Hudson 491 (previous page) with unstreamlined 492 built as a heavy Pacific. C&O's class F-19 Pacific of 1926 (490-494) was the apex of the 4-6-2 type. As Phil Shuster wrote, it "compared closely with the Pennsy's K-4, the B&O's P-7, and Southern's PS-4 Pacific types." Photo is undated and unlocated. A good guess is in early 1930s at Washington, D.C. The "eagle" 492 is intended for C&O's premier train, the *George Washington*, as sign on tender designates.

E. L. Huddleston

When in 1946-47 the five F-19 Pacifics were streamlined, they were actually almost completely rebuilt. No. 494 was left without a jacket when plans for Chessie folded. Thus one can see some of the very modern features that new L-1 Hudson, no. 494, discloses at Ashland in 1947, chief among them being the Franklin Type "A" poppet valves, the extra lubricator behind the cylinders, the front-end throttle, and the roller bearing main and side rods.

E. L. Huddleston
Left side view of L-1 Hudson no. 494 at Hinton westbound in 1948 reveals big pipe headed to trailer booster, bell under headlight, and generator over no. 2 driver.

E. L. Huddleston, C&O Historical Society collection
Rear of tender for L-1 Hudson 490 (stored dead at Huntington in 1957) reads "28 tons, 18,000 gals." Fluting on the tender hood matches precisely the style and measurements of the fluting on the Budd-built stainless steel coaches purchased for *Chessie*.

E. L. Huddleston
New Budd Co. stainless steel dome car 1852 (one of three for Chessie) displayed at Huntington was the first on any railroad east of the Mississippi. In dome was seating for 24. Downstairs were "cabins" intended for the crew, plus train operations center, and drawing rooms configured for daytime passenger use.

E. L. Huddleston

The eastbound F.F.V. (winter of 1946-47), a heavy-weight coach and Pullman train, leaves Russell, Ky., behind Hudson no. 490, which makes just as forceful exhaust as a steamer with conventional piston valves, but which emits the exhaust in more rapidly formed individual puffs of smoke and steam with multiple poppet valves, that open and close like automotive valves.

J. H. Dean, Ray Curl collection

Ten Wheelers (4-6-0) were a popular type at the turn of the century. All four Pocahontas roads had Ten-Wheelers, especially plentiful on C&O. Two of the most esthetically pleasing classes C&O had came from roads absorbed. No. 377 (blt. 1902) on display at Baltimore, came from the Cincinnati, Richmond [Ind.] and Muncie, by way of the CC & L, which C&O bought. The other fine 4-6-0, built 1910 for the Hocking Valley Railroad in Ohio, went to C&O when it took over the HV. On July 16, 1931 at Columbus, Ohio, C&O F-12 no. 88 (retaining its HV number) shows its sleek lines.

Ten-Wheelers came in all shapes and sizes as comparison of the three classes of 4-6-0s pictured in this book attests. C&O's ex-Hocking Valley 4-6-0s were built as passenger engines and to make speed with 73-inch drivers. They looked especially up-to-date after the slide valves were replaced by piston valves on the main cylinders. No. 89 rests at Athens, Ohio around 1946 with the daily train to Columbus.

C&O no. 90 (ex-Hocking Valley 4-6-0) runs over ex-HV along Ohio River between Chesire and Hobson Yard, Ohio, circa 1947. This train, originating at Pomeroy, is 76.3 miles from Columbus as bridge number indicates. The hill and dale scenery of the Appalachian Plateau Province persists to Lancaster, Ohio, where glaciation made for flatter land forms. (Norfolk Southern now controls this stretch of track.)

E. L. Huddleston

With the slow attrition of the steam locomotive following end of World War II, many fans were motivated to set up excursions with steamers saved from scrapping. That happened to Black Mountain Ten-Wheeler no. 1. (Official Guide of 1959 lists this CRR subsidiary as ten and a half miles long, connecting with the CRR at Kona, N. C.) This light 4-6-0, built in 1882, was put to work on excursion trains in 1968, and in 1979 was donated to the B&O Museum in Baltimore. In 1957, before restoration, it rests on the "dead line" at CRR's motive power headquarters at Erwin, TN.

Everett N. Young

At the Breaks of the Sandy, crossing spectacular Pool Point bridge, CRR no. 1 (CRR once owned no. 1) heads back to Kingsport with excursion April 27, 1975. An attractive "cow catcher" has replaced the ungainly footboard-pilot combination seen while in storage at Erwin. Diesel helpers behind no. 1 are doing the actual hauling up the steep grade.

The limit for the restored CRR Ten Wheeler was 2 cars, so diesels usually assisted on its scenic runs. In 1968 Bob Harvey of Kingsport caught no. 1 southbound crossing 801 ft. Boones Creek viaduct in the Great Valley, fourth longest bridge on the Clinchfield.

E. L. Huddleston
The importance of the Logan County coal field to the C&O is illustrated by the Company's running a special train from Huntington to Logan on the 100th anniversary of the founding of Logan in 1852. By 1952 old C&O steam engines were hard to find. Nos. 377 and 378, built in 1902, had operated until 1951 on the light-railed Craig Valley Subdivision in Virginia. The Huntington main locomotive shops did a good job of "shopping," for 377 operated under steam into the 1970s. Purists would point out that in 1902 377 had no power reverse gear (under middle of running board). Period head lamp looks very authentic; it must have been in storage somewhere!

E. L. Huddleston
The special run to Logan that September morning, 1952, did not replace the regularly scheduled local, which usually had a light Pacific as power (replaced around this time by a Brill gas-electric). Today the local has a big Berkshire (or Kanawha, as known on C&O) in the lead, as no. 377 waits to back onto its train after the local clears the station.

E. L. Huddleston
Ten-wheeler no. 377 has backed to its train at the Huntington depot, and awaits departure Sept. 9, 1952, for Logan Centennial. The train imitates the first to head up the Guyandotte, in September 1904. Caboose for this run was 90382, built in 1882; other cars included hopper-bottom gondola built for the Sandy Valley and Elkhorn (a road taken over by C&O in 1933), a period box car, and a wooden sheathed orange passenger-baggage combine no. 417.

E. L. Huddleston
Russell, Ky., celebrated its own Centennial in 1978, and The *Chessie Steam Special* pulled an excursion from Columbus to Russell and back to help celebrate it. Pulled by 2101, an ex-Reading Railroad 4-8-4. In 1945-47 the Reading Railroad sucessfully rebuilt Consolidations (2-8-0) into Norhterns with 70 inch drivers. Northern 2101 hauled the popular *Chessie Steam Specials* in 1977-78 until it was burned up during winter storage late in 1978. 2101 has backed its train from the Russell depot to get to the outside, or passenger, main and engineer Ross Rowland now opens the throttle wide (this engine never seemed to slip) and closes cylinder cocks as the long and crowded train heads back to Columbus late in the afternoon while two trains wait to enter the yard.

> *"The hauling of coal from mine to yards and from*
> *yard to destination involved combinations of grade,*
> *curvature and tonnage, which only a powerful and*
> *flexible locomotive could manage."*
>
> —Robert A. LeMassena in
> *Articulated Steam Locomotives of North America*

Writing about life in the present is not much fun because life as we live it is so fluid and hard to understand. Many of us find the past more fulfilling to write about because we can see the past in a more balanced perspective than the present. We can "put a handle on it" as the saying goes, due to commentaries by experts who size up the past and who fix in time people, events, the arts, and technology. We think they know what this phenomena mean. Understanding what's going on in regard to locomotives in America is a case in point. Sorting out today's models (due to their similarities in specifications and appearance) is difficult even though only two manufacturers make diesels for American railroads. (Does the average railfan know the difference between General Electric's models C30-7 and C44-8W?) There are a lot more easily understood differences among this variety if one goes back to, say, the period between World War I and the end of steam (mostly in the 1950s). Getting a handle on individual U.S. railroads was a lot easier then than now, for railroads had names that associated them with particular parts of the country, like Baltimore and Ohio. Today the huge systems still around after the mega mergers have names that mean very little–like giant Burlington Northern Santa Fe (known fondly as BNSF) or Norfolk Southern or CSX. As Freeman Hubbard once pointed out, CSX is a formula signifying "Chessie System" multiplied by the unknown quantity "X." Nothing replaced Chessie the cat as a logo when CSX was created. In that particular, Norfolk Southern is ahead of CSX, for it adopted an unnamed, prancing thoroughbred racehorse as its logo. Only Union Pacific is a name that reconciles the present with the past, for that name is appropriate for a railroad that stretches almost across a continent today and one that goes back to the true "Wild West" days right after the end of the Civil War.

Because the past has been so well studied, there are workable frameworks for understanding the flux of events in time. In trying to understand the motive power situation of the four roads that are the subject of this book, one can use a threefold framework that gives an overview at once logical but not exhausted by repetition in other recent American locomotive histories; namely, the locomotive types in largest number, the most powerful, and the most modern.

It is not surprising that Mallets (articulated locomotives) are most numerous on these four heavy- tonnage and stiff -grade "mountain" railroads. Mallets, named after their European inventor (and pronounced "Malleys"), have two engines under one firebox and boiler. When first developed, Mallets only used compound expansion; that is, steam exhausted from the rear engine went to the front engine. Over a decade later, boilers and fire boxes were made big enough that they could supply high-pressure steam equally to both engines (called single expansion).

Added together, the 2-6-6-2 Mallet totaled the highest on the four roads, but the 2-8-8-2 Mallet dominated as the one design used in common on three of the roads The reason that 2-6-6-2s were more numerous than 2-8-8-2s was that from not until after time of their introduction to 1918 did N&W develop a 2-8-8-2 that would surpass in performance its 2-6-6-2s. C&O owned a huge fleet of 2-6-6-2s because not until the 1920's did C&O figure out a way to use 2-8-8-2s in C&O's narrow tunnels. C&O 2-6-6-2s (and the 190 N&W copies) were outstanding designs, for, besides being superheated, they were equipped with a combustion chamber ahead of the firebox (nearly 7 ft. long) to give room for more complete combustion, and the roomy firebox sat completely behind the last driver, the first Mallets so designed.

It should be noted that all four roads had 2-8-8-2s. However, the N&W, Virginian, and Clinchfield had compound 2-8-8-2s (the true Mallets); C&O's 2-8-8-2s were "simple" articulateds, which were not supposed to be called Mallets, but most employees did anyway. C&O had been unable to use compound 2-8-8-2s because their dimension exceeded tunnel clearances at the time. (Collis Huntington, in financing the building of the C&O's mainline through the mountains was rather stingy in allocating money for construction.) C&O developed the 2-8-8-2 as a simple articulated (that is with high pressure steam going directly to both sets of cylinders) in order to solve the problem that its tunnels posed in using big power.

N&W 1444, built by Alco in 1916, was one of 190 2-6-6-2 Mallets N&W received over six years from 1912 to 1918. In 1947 this 2-6-6-2, at Kenova, W.Va., is returning C&O interchange cars at KV interlocking.Emissions control device on smoke stack is evidence that this engine has worked in Cincinnati area, which had strict smoke abatement laws.

"brass" of the USRA than any other Pocahontas road. Its motive power department was represented by John Pilcher's serving on the USRA design committee and its own president served as Regional manager. The USRA heavy Mallet as developed was a modified and improved version of N&W's own 2-8-8-2 of 1918. However, both the Virginian and the Clinchfield felt the USRA was assigning them engines smaller and less powerful than those each road could handle. The

If 2-6-6-2s predominated when added up on three roads (the Virginian had no 2-6-6-2s), the 2-8-8-2s predominated as a single type, and that type was the "heavy" Mallet developed by the United States Railroad Administration as one of its twelve standard designs established when the federal government took over the nation's railroads at the start of World War I. Because time between placing an order and getting a new locomotive was about nine months, all 2-8-8-2s assigned by USRA to the mountain carriers came in 1919, after the War was over. C&O was assigned "government" Mallets, too, in 1919 but they were the "light" Mallet–the 2-6-6-2, since C&O's main-line clearances were too restrictive for the bigger Mallet.

Both models of USRA Mallets had 57-inch drivers, so both were quite suitable for hauling heavy coal loads out of Appalachia, and that is probably the reason that all original USRA Mallets were allotted to coal carriers—C&O with 30 2-6-6-2s, Wheeling and Lake Erie with 10 2-6-6-2s, N&W with 50 2-8-8-2s, Virginian with 20 2-8-8-2s and Clinchfield with 10 2-8-8-2s. How willing were the roads to take power they had no hand in picking? N&W had the least objections because one could say this road got exactly what it wanted. It had more influence with the top

Virginian went as far as refusing its first allotment of 2-8-8-2s by the USRA. This road felt that because of (in Lloyd D. Lewis's words) the road's "liberal line clearances and heavy permissible axle loading," its 2-8-8-2s of 1912-13 and especially its 2-10-10-2s of 1918 could not be surpassed as mountain maulers. (The Virginian, later forced to accept an allocation of 2-8-8-2s, discovered they performed better than they had expected).

The Clinchfield accepted its allocation of ten but this road also believed it deserved a bigger locomotive. This is made clear in an item in *Railway Review* for 1919 noting CRR's receipt of seven 2-8-8-2s of its own design. The item declares that the CRR's new 2-8-8-2 Mallets (class L-1) exceeded in vertical and horizontal clearance the government standardized design, the former being a foot taller than the latter. Nevertheless, the CRR must have liked the USRA design (class L-2) better than its own, for when in the booming 1920s it needed more big power, it bought copies of the USRA 2-8-8-2s instead of it own. Also, it stored its own class L-1's for much of the Great Depression. Still, the Clinchfield could not admit the government engines were as good as they actually were, since the were a foot shorter than the Clinchfield's own 2-8-8-2s. Thus when Clinchfield

Playing the numbers game

In both drawbar horsepower and potential boiler horsepower, the C&O and Virginian 2-6-6-6 type (called Blue Ridge on VGN and Allegheny on C&O) is the winner. Data on drawbar horsepower measured in service is covered in *Lima's Finest* (Hundman Publishing) and *World's Greatest Steam Locomotives* (TLC). Table showing "potential horsepower" of some representative modern steam locomotives is in appendix to his treatise on the steam locomotive published in 1942 and revised in 1944 by Ralph Johnson, chief engineer at Baldwin during the end of the Super Power era following World War II. Johnson writes, " The commonly used horsepower rating for steam locomotives is based on the boiler." He adds that of the many formulas available, the simplest is: calculated evaporation per hour divided by steam per indicated horsepower-hour gives potential horsepower. "This is based," he says, "on the assumption that the steaming capacity of the boiler is proportional to the total heating surface and that sufficient fuel can be fired to push the steam production to the limit set by the heating surface. ...The evaporation per hour is calculated from the heating surface of the boiler and certain empirical values of evaporation per square foot of direct and indirect heating surfaces. ...The steam used per indicated horsepower-hour, or the efficiency of the transformation of the potential-energy of the steam into useful work is dependent in the main on two factors: (1) boiler pressure; (2) degrees of superheat."

Calculations of potential horsepower for 15 representative types are in Johnson's table of "Typical Locomotive Proportions," of which six are articulateds. Ranked from highest potential horsepower to lowest in the table, they are: (1) C&O class H-8 (2-6-6-6) of 1941, at 6980 HP; (2) Duluth, Missabe, and Iron Range class M-3 (2-8-8-4) of 1941 at 6801 HP; (3) Western Pacific class M-137-151 (2-8-8-2) of 1931 at 6463 HP; (4) Western Maryland class M-2 (4-6-6-4) of 1941 at 6345; (5) Union Pacific class 4000 (4-8-8-4) of 1941 at 6167; and Seaboard Air Line class R-1 (2-6-6-4) of 1935 at 4877. The layman would say that what is being measured here is the volume of steam the boiler is capable of producing!

E. L. Huddleston

In 1918, N&W stopped buying 2-6-6-2 Mallets and started buying 2-8-8-2 Mallets in a big way. No. 2051 was the second engine of a 1923 order for compound articulateds copied from plans for the 50 USRA "heavy Mallets" of standardized design allotted to N&W during the period of federal control of the railroads in World War I. By this date, 1959, at East Portsmouth, Ohio, no. 2051 no longer works on the road but in the yard, evidenced by footboards instead of "cow catcher." Sister engine no. 2050 is displayed at Illinois Railway Museum at Union, Ill.

C&O Historical Society collection

C&O plus Wheeling and Lake Erie were the only roads to receive the USRA "light Mallet" type (2-6-6-2). No copies were ever built. This is in sharp contrast to the USRA heavy Mallets, for N&W, Clinchfield, and Virginian, all having received original allotments, came back for copies. This official USRA builders photo shows that the 20 C&O Mallets were delivered with road style pilots and only one air pump.

E. L. Huddleston
C&O USRA 2-6-6-2 Mallet no. 1538, in 1951, shoves eastbound coal train up the 0.3% grade of Scary Hill west of Milton, West Virginia. A 2-8-4 is on the head end. Besides renumbering and building a larger cab for the crew's comfort, C&O did not make a lot of changes to the to these Mallets.

ordered its ten copies of the USRA engines (four years after the USRA ceased to exist) it made sure the new engines, while preserving the basic specifications of the originals, had bigger cabs, bigger and higher domes on top of the boiler, and higher smoke stacks. These clearance modifications told the world that the Clinchfield, though built through the mountains, had, like the Virginian Railway, quite "liberal line clearances." The important thing about the "government" heavy Mallets was that all three roads getting them, despite their complaints about the originals, placed more orders for them after government control ended.

The C&O did not willingly take the 2-6-6-2's USRA allotted it. The road's official position was reported in *Railway Review* for August 23, 1919: "During the year the railroad administration notified your company there had been allotted to it twenty-five freight and passenger locomotives...Directors of your company were of the opinion that the equipment so allocated was not necessary to the efficient operation of the railroad, that much of it was unsuited for your company's purposes and that the purchase of such equipment... was inadvisable." C&O felt it did not need them because the road already had a fleet of fine performing 2-6-6-2s and was by 1918 looking for bigger power for its mainline mountain crossing. Problem is, it could not take the 2-8-8-2s for use up the New River and over the Allegheny summit, because of tunnel clearances. C&O's mainline had been constructed about twenty-five years before the Virginian's and Clinchfield's , and drilling and blasting techniques were still relatively primitive. Also, the financier building the C&O westward out of Virginia did not want to spend any more than necessary; costs were already high enough just getting a line through the New River Gorge. Thus tunnel clearances were kept to a minimum. So C&O could take only the smaller Mallet, the 2-6-6-2. Having to accept them so rankled C&O that it never used the USRA 2-6-6-2s over its mainline mountain divisions. Naturally, it never ordered any copies! So unpopular among railroad management was the government takeover that C&O's negativism was typical of railroads

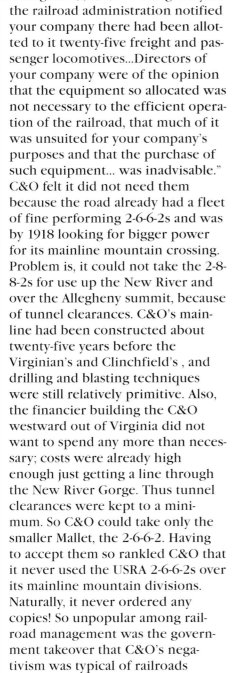

receiving government locomotives, even though all twelve designs were quite well engineered.

C&O solved the problem of clearances (until a 1930's tunnel reconstruction program) by working with Alco to produce a powerful "Mallet" that would stay within its clearances. This was also a 2-8-8-2, but the H-7 had a new type of steam distribution system keeping it from designation as a true "Mallet." The steam went directly from boiler to both front and rear engines. Sending steam directly doubled the requirement for steam; thus a big boiler was needed. The new "simple" 2-8-8-2s had the longest boiler yet fabricated by American Locomotive Company, having five separate courses exclusive of the section over the firebox. The boiler's maximum outside diameter--104 inches--was outstanding for such a long boiler. To meet clearances with such a big boiler, the height of the locomotive was carefully controlled. Maximum height at the stack was fifteen ft. even. (Maximum height of the USRA compound 2-8-8-2 was 15 ft., 6 inches.) C&O employees called these engines "Simons;" (short for Simple Simon); officially the company designated the H-7 and H-7 as "Chesapeakes" but the name never took hold.

Prior to this "simple" locomotive, all articulateds had been compounds; afterwards, most were simple. Another advantage of the simple over compound was that the front set of cylinders on a "simple" articulated were the same size as the rear; on the compound, cylinder size often tested the limits of horizontal clearances. The only significant development of the true Mallet thereafter was the N&W's Y-6 class, which took the basic USRA 2-8-8-2 and improved on it to achieve significant gains in tractive effort and horsepower over the period from 1919 to 1952.

There is no controversy in picking out the most numerous type of road freight locomotives on the four roads. More controversial is naming the most powerful of all . That is because power can be measured in two principal ways. Tractive effort, or starting power, is calculated by a formula that allows 15% loss in pressure between steam pressure developed in the boiler and steam that actually gets to work on the face of the piston. With modern locomotives the loss could be less than 15%, an arbitrary figure apparently. Thus, to get more precise measurement of a steamer's starting power required measurement of the drawbar pull at the coupler on the tender. Horsepower can also be calculated, and projected on a graph. But , again, horsepower as measured at the tender drawbar was the most reliable. Both drawbar measurements required a dynamometer car for field testing the locomotive in question.

Most powerful in tractive effort were the ten 2-10-10-2s built by the Virginian in 1918. According to R. A. LeMassena, "At very low speed the tractive effort was 176,000 lbs., while above 5 mph in compound-mode it was 117,000 lbs." Because it could not long operate

N&W liked the USRA 2-8-8-2s so much it started making its own copies at its Roanoke locomotive shops, like class Y-5 no. 2105. Visible improvements in appliances include low water alarm device and front-end throttle. Though impressive in size, the USRA 2-8-8-2 had diminutive trailer truck (under cab). Engine terminal scene is at Auville yard, Iaeger.

in simple, tractive effort in compound was the meaningful measure of power Of course, they were so slow as to test the patience of the crew if they were used east of Roanoke, where 20 mph might be their speed at full throttle in compound. These big engines are mysterious, for few really good pictures of them in action seem to exist. This writer almost saw two in action. This occurred when as a sixteen-year-old he implored his uncle, whom he was visiting in Beckley, W.Va., to drive him down to Mullens so he could see some of the monstrous Mallets. I recall my uncle letting me drive most of the way, for I had just gotten my driver's license (but did not have my own car). At Mullens (more particularly Elmore yards along the banks of the Guyandotte River) my uncle left me in the car and crossed the footbridge to the yardmaster's office. There he learned that a couple of the 2-10-10-2s were up the "hill" assisting the box-cab "motors" in

moving the previous day's tonnage to the top of the Appalachian plateau west of Princeton. In retrospect this seems a very inefficient operation, for the Company had to use a mix of steam and electric power in getting the coal out of the level of the Guyandotte to the summit of Flattop Mountain. Apparently the grade was so steep that the D.C. electrics in themselves could not move in one train enough tonnage to make the move worthwhile. (Or else the company was short of electric locomotives.)

With no promise of them coming back to Elmore soon, I started photographing what was in the terminal, including box-cab "motors" and a couple of Mikados. The most interesting find of the day was what was being used on the hump engine (which was idle at that time)—a 2-8-8-2 that had been made at the Princeton Shops by taking the boiler and firebox of the ill-fated "Triplex" Mallet and putting a regular

In 1923, Clinchfield bought copies of its own "government" allotted 2-8-8-2s, but did not want observers to think of them as copies, so it modified the domes, cab, and stack to make them bigger. No. 739 is at Erwin, Tennessee, September 11, 1947. Note "cubby-hole" for head brakeman, left front of tender.

Mallet "chassis" under it. (The Triplex was an attempt to use steam three times, the third engine being under the tender). Needless to say, the home-made 2-8-8-2 (which had first come from Princeton Shops as a 2-8-8-0) had a huge boiler, but even that "fat" boiler had not supplied enough steam to make the Triplex work out in practice.) .

Most powerful in horsepower, as measured by a dynamometer car manufactured by Baldwin Locomotive Works, was the 2-6-6-6 type, first built for the C&O in 1941 and copied by the Virginian in 1945. So much has been written about this locomotive that it is unnecessary to review the statistics and the close competition with its rivals for title of most powerful. Anecdotal evidence alone convinces this writer. His own I might add! When a 2-6-6-6 was at full throttle and running, say, in the 25-30 mph range, with maximum tonnage on an ever so slight upgrade, what one observed was almost an explosion coming out the twin smokestacks. The cascading steam and spent fuel erupted with rocket-like force with a sound to match. And if he could have looked inside the firebox of any modern steam locomotive, he would have observed "a perfect cyclone of combustion," in the words of R. S. Henry in *This Fascinating Railroad Business...* "An engine working at capacity," he added, "changes the entire gaseous content of its firebox from seven to ten times every second." And confirming the intensity of the firebox inferno are the words of Ralph Johnson, Baldwin's chief engineer: In tests, the velocity of gases passing over the firebox arch and into the combustion chamber (measured on Pennsylvania M-1a Mountain type) reached 263 m.p.h. No wonder a look through the firedoor could be frightening!

The most modern steam locomotive design for all the four roads cannot be established since any steam locomotive built after 1934 could be considered modern because by that time the solid cast-steel engine frame had been perfected and roller bearings developed that would bear a locomotive's weight. About

the only significant development that would come after these was the poppet valve (Franklin System of Steam Distribution). Designating the most modern freight locomotive on each road is fairly easy and without controversy. On the Virginian it would be the 2-8-4 and 2-6-6-6 from Lima Locomotive Works in 1945 and 1946. But complicating the choice on the Virginian was that the portion of the main line that had the steepest mountain grades had been electrified with overhead wires ever since 1925-26. The EL-C "motors" of 1956-57 came from General Electric and were quite modern (ignitron rectifier type) but hardly attractive. They were, of course, the Virginian's newest engines.

Norfolk and Western also had the most mountainous portion of its main line electrified. But the road tore down the wires and went back to steam in 1950! Heavily trafficked N&W was forced to electrify its Flattop Mountain crossing as early as 1916, simply because the close confines of the tunnel at the summit suffocated crews and it took "forever" to get through it on the upgrade. Miraculously, steam came back to Elkhorn Mountain (as the eastward grade up Elkhorn Creek was called) when N&W constructed a new tunnel in 1950. Although considerably longer than the old summit tunnel, the new tunnel was on a lower alignment and had much more liberal clearances. In addition, a huge fan could blow the smoke out of the tunnel ahead of the lead locomotive, which was usually a Y6 class 2-8-8-2. After World War II, N&W faced a dilemma. Its jack-shaft electric locomotives were aging and needed replacement. Foreseeing abandonment of electrification, N&W ordered no new "motors" in the post-war years. N&W's electric locomotives, unlike the Virginian's, were not in the contest for most modern.

The Clinchfield, having no "catenary," has only one nomination for most modern–the four 4-6-6-4 Challenger types of 1947, strongly influenced in design and styling by the Delaware and Hudson Challengers of 1940-1942. To gather data on these

H. Reid

View from inside Virginian engine house in August 1950 at Elmore yard shows three USRA type 2-8-82 Mallets and a Mike (2-8-2) plus cinder pit and monumental coaling station.

engines, Clinchfield officials went up to Schenectady, New York, to confer with Alco and then a few miles away to the operating headquarters of the Delaware and Hudson at Albany. Why Clinchfield had Challengers is hard to understand. They seemed out of place on a road that had lots of "dead" freight to haul—namely coal—that would not be run at speeds above 40 mph very often. They were also out of place because, as Ken Marsh points out, the Clinchfield "did not have any flat territory." It was "always climbing or descending." George Drury in his guide to steam locomotives says, "At the beginning of World War II the Clinchfield needed locomotives that could pull like the 2-8-8-2s and run like the Mikados." This implies that the big USRA designed 2-8-8-2s were slow moving and the 2-8-2s were speedy but not as powerful. Obviously. Mr. Drury, as astute observer of American steam power, must want us to conclude that the Clinchfield desired speed and power combined. That may be true.

Because the first order of CRR 4-6-6-4s was formalized in 1941 (and delivered in 1942-43) they were not under control of the War Production Board, which controlled industrial output. Thus CRR had free reign to get whatever kind of articulated it wanted. One suspects that just as Clinchfield had been sensitive about its locomotive orders back in World War I, it was still that way in World War II. Therefore, the CRR did not want to imitate the Virginian, C&O,

or N&W. The best way to assert its independence was to adopt an articulated with a four-wheel leading truck. All its Pocahontas competitors had studiously avoided four-wheel leading trucks on their modern steam freight locomotives. (N&W had a fleet of 4-8-0 freight engines but they dated back to 1906-1912.) To give its 4-6-6-4s more tractive power, the CRR increased the bore of the cylinders an inch and a half over the D&H models and put more weight on the drivers.

The Clinchfield had three groups of Challengers, a type that by the way, had been "invented" by the Union Pacific, where fast running in the "Big Sky" country of the far West was necessary because of the vast distances covered. First came eight E-1 4-6-6-4s modeled on the Delaware and Hudson's own 4-6-6-4s. Then, in the middle of the War, the War Production Board–requiring use of an existing design for orders under ten– diverted some Challengers of Union Pacific design to the Denver and Rio Grande Western, which having 4-6-6-4s of its own design, did not want but was forced by the WPB to take. The six orphans, through the War Assets Administration, eventually ended up on the Clinchfield in 1947. On account of a power shortage, CRR took these 4-6-6-4s, quite similar in design and appearance to the famous Union Pacific "Jabelman" Challengers of 1942-1944. In 1947 American Locomotive Works made for the Clinchfield four more Challengers based on the original D&H

design; and they were Alco's last articulateds.

In looking at pictures of the two groups of articulateds-- the D&H-CRR design and the Union Pacific-D&RGW-CRR design, one notes a significant difference: namely, the Union Pacific engines, which the D&RGW was forced to take during the War, had a huge cover over the smokestack lacking on the D&H engines. In fact, closer examination discloses that the Union Pacific Challengers had two big smoke stacks hidden by the cover (which served as mount for a retractable "smoke hood") whereas the D&H design had but one stack. Even more examination (inside the smokebox!) would disclose the UP engines had an exhaust nozzle configuration quite different from the "Master Mechanics front end" on the D&H machines. When the CRR put into service the

E. L. Huddleston

This impressive single expansion, simple articulated class A, no. 1234, has stopped in Ironton, Ohio, in November, 1953, and almost immediately thereafter has started up again with a vengeance. The engineer has opened the throttle with a rapid, single motion, for before that first big blast from the stack, the engine was straining at every seam, evidenced by a sudden steam leak in the front sleeve joint. It then accelerated its long train of empty hoppers and took off almost literally. Especially stylish with the air after-cooler grid below the headlight, 1234 has a look of authority.

Challengers with nozzles of UP design, it discovered they did not perform well on Eastern coal. Thus CRR altered the front end to eliminate both the double stacks and the smoke hood and substituted a more conventional Master Mechanics configuration. And according to Ken Marsh, the "pinhole" grates in the fire box were replaced with "finger" grates more suitable for burning high BTU Eastern coal.

Most modern steam locomotive on the Norfolk and Western would have to be steam-turbo-electric no. 2300, built by Baldwin-Westinghouse in 1954. It was steam power's last, best hope. However, it was never duplicated and N&W gave in to conventional diesel-electrics, leading to the scrapping of this turbine nicknamed "Jawn Henry" in 1957. Conventional steamers on N&W were being built as late as 1952 and 1953 in the company's own big locomotive shops in Roanoke, Virginia, headquarters for the road.

The most modern conventional design to emerge from the Company's shops was the Class A of 1936—a simple articulated with 70-inch drivers. At the time this engine was designed and built, in the middle of the Great Depression, it took lots of guts to go out on a limb, design-wise, and introduce high driving wheels. While the Seaboard 2-6-6-4, appearing one year before the N&W's, had 69-inch drivers, it had

neither the grate area nor boiler girth to produce steam in great enough volume to take advantage of those high drivers with a big load. Just think of it–96 sq. ft. grate area on the SAL articulated and 122 sq. ft. on the N&W class A. The N&W class A (2-6-6-4) also deserves plaudits for introducing to the world the first truly modern Super Power articulated. True, it did not pioneer the 2-6-6-4 type (never given a name) because the Pittsburgh and West Virginia introduced a 2-6-6-4 simple articulated in 1934. However, even though this good looking steamer had a respectable grate area (102 sq. ft.) it had only 63-inch drivers. The Union Pacific Challenger type (4-6-6-4) , introduced in 1936 just two months after N&W's first 2-6-6-4, was truly Super Power but it was not pioneering because unlike the N&W articulateds the early Challengers had neither roller bearings for the driving wheels nor Commonwealth cast-steel frames integrating the cylinders. Also, the Challengers had less starting tractive effort than the class A and less horsepower. Corresponding to N&W's development of a Super Power articulated was its designing in its Roanoke Shops an exceptionally big and speedy passenger locomotive right before war broke out. The world-famous class J 4-8-4 passenger engine has been covered in detail in Ken Miller's recent book on the J.

Although they could not be considered modern

in their designs being of recent origin, like the classes A and J, the N&W 0-8-0s and "improved" 2-8-8-2s are modern in that in that N&W refined their performances so that they were in the forefront of steam locomotive designs. Both originated when the USRA devised standardized steam locomotives for the nation's railroads during World War I. The designs were so good, however, that they were imitated numerous times in the 1920's, 1930's and up to 1944. In the case of the 0-8-0 and 2-8-8-2 they were not only copied, they were improved with accessories, minor dimensional changes, and construction features that made them modern. The N&W ended up with 75 of the improved 0-8-0s, 30 of them coming from C&O which, having purchased them new from Baldwin in late 1948, then decided to diesel immediately. The famed Y-6 series climaxed with the 30 classy Y-6b's of 1948-1952. These were improved USRA 2-8-8-2s that N&W had first received as class Y-3 in 1919, totaling 50 from Baldwin and Alco. By 1952, then, N&W owned 50 original USRA Mallets and 141 improved. They were ubiquitous mountain locomotives, being used on the mainline as lead engines and pushers and on branches as mine shifters.

N&W kept building and buying 0-8-0s and 2-8-8-2s until December, 1953. C&O (which had never needed electrics) reached a climax in orders in 1948. The road was on a "roll" that year with new steam power. However, a drastic inflation of the operating ratio caused C&O management to look for ways to economize. The entrenched officials of C&O's Mechanical Department or its depleted Advisory Mechanical Committee were not about to tell upper management that the whole structure of locomotive maintenance and operation would be permanently changed for the better by diesels. C&O management got direction for what to do from the Pere Marquette District of the C&O, which had been merged into C&O in 1947 and which was well

Harold K. Vollrath

C&O could not use USRA 2-8-8-2s through the Appalachians because its tunnels were not built with clearances looking forward to bigger and better equipment. A tunnel enlargement and elimination project of the early 1930s finally permitted the biggest Super Power. To meet the challenge of the 1920s, C&O and Alco designed a 2-8-8-2 that could supply steam directly to two engines, unlike the USRA 2-8-8-2s. By the time of photo of 1558 in 1938 at Hinton, the front sand dome had been enlarged and the stack height increased. The big "Simons" (name given by railroaders) reward study of every detail, especially the older cold water pump for the Elesco feedwater heater, the ladder under firebox, and walkway over front cylinders.

E. L. Huddleston

By 1947, most of the "Simons" had been sold to Union Pacific for war service and to RF&P for hump service. The few 2-8-8-2 simple articulateds remaining on C&O were in hump service, like 1572 at Russell, or in pusher service at the Sciotoville bridge. 1572, equipped with retrofitted air after-coolers, awaits hump duty near old YMCA.

into diesel usage because of its close association with General Motors and the auto industry. Anyway, in that last year (and on into 1949) before the ax fell on C&O steam. the road received new Hudsons, the world's heaviest 4-6-4 passenger locomotives, new 4-8-4s, called Greenbriers on C&O, new switchers (as reported above) and new simple articulateds, the remarkable 2-6-6-6s, which would now total 60.

Last, but certainly not least were 10 (cut down from an original order for 25) new 2-6-6-2s for mine run service, based on a World War I design very simi-

Norfolk and Western
N&W tried to save the coal burning steam locomotive by an electric transmission (from Westinghouse) and a watertube "flash" boiler with 600 psi pressure. Completed in 1954, no. 2300 was powered by 12 traction motors. In a publicity picture, "Jawn Henry" (as nicknamed) starts down grade from the summit of the Alleghenies at Christiansburg, Va. with 10,000 tons of eastbound coal.

lar to the design of the standardized 2-6-6-2 devised by the USRA. Some locomotive historians find it hard to understand how the last engines built in the United States by a commercial manufacturer should be copies of a World War I design. The class H-6, nos. 1300-1309, were copies, true enough, but the original H-4 and H-6 C&O 2-6-6-6s were fine locomotives that could pull anything (I've seen them working in "simple" at walking speed) and keep their footing on sharp curves and they could be operated on branches with restrictive clearances. They were, of course, the models for the USRA 2-6-6-2s, and the ten that arrived in 1949 had refinements like front-end throttles and over-fire air jets. Also arriving in 1949 were three new switchers from Porter Locomotive Works that went to work at the Union Carbide and Carbon Chemical complex at South Charleston, West Virginia. These three 0-6-0 F's had no firebox to spread cinders that might ignite a fire at the chemical plant. Rather they

were insulated like a thermos bottle and received a charge of superheated water from stationary boilers at the plant, enough to keep them operating for a shift. That C&O bought these engines demonstrates how suddenly the road gave up its commitment to steam-power, for not long after they went to work in West Virginia, C&O started assigning its new Alco S-2 switchers to various yards around the system.

As for a survey of diesels on the four Pocahontas roads, that subject gets too complex to handle here, for one has to cover numerous manufacturers—Alco-GE, GE alone, Fairbanks-Morse, Baldwin, Baldwin-Lima-Hamilton, and Electro-Motive Division of General Motors--not to mention numerous models. My knowledge of diesels is limited mostly to the C&O, for that is the road I have followed closely. At the beginning--that is, the early 1950s—C&O tried to spread its diesel orders around, buying road switchers from both Alco-GE and Baldwin (later Baldwin-

Lima-Hamilton after the merger of BLW with Lima). However, General Motors, with its big plant in the Chicago suburbs, got most of the orders. I recently came across an evaluation of diesels by manufacturer and model that rings true to what I have heard over the years. C&O started out with the GM "carbody" E and F units, as well as the hood units in the GP7 and GP9 model series and then graduated to, among other "second generation" models, the U30Cs, and, of course, later the EMD SD40-2s—all of which models are mentioned in this evaluation taking diesel development up to the present .

Mrs. Voight, editor of an R&LHS regional publication, writes in the national R&LHS Newsletter (Vol 21, Autumn 2001) first of the Alco-GE and Fairbanks-Morse products, the former of which gave "a string of problems" and the latter of which "simply did not make a good product." (She does not mention Baldwin, however.) Despite some comfort problems, she likes the early EMDs: "Carbody controls [on E and F units] were too awkward for the engineer to reach and the cab noise was terrible, since cab and engine shared the same housing. Hood units finally displaced the Fs though many of both had been built in the same '49-'53 time span. The hood locomotives [GP7 and GP9] were almost like 'Cadillacs' compared to the carbodies, someone observed. Later and larger EMD GPs and SDs delighted enginemen, especially the SD40-2, probably the most versatile, easy to handle, brilliantly conceived of all DC-traction diesel-electrics. EMD had just about cornered the road-engine market, while for a few decades GE [after ending its association with Alco] attempted a successful invasion with its U-series

diesels. For some reason they [GE] remained confined within the limits of 1960's technology. U30Cs, U28Cs, U25Cs, etc as well as four-axle models were poorly received... The gist of GE's early efforts was captured by an engineer with 38 years of service on the Santa Fe: An EMD has a GE beat by a city block..." She further notes that advocates for GE claimed that a U-boat [U25B] could "dig in" and "deliver more tractive effort starting out with a train than a comparable EMD. But these advocates failed to take into account "old-timers who noticed that the Us [U-model types

from GE] aged very, very rapidly when given that most arduous of dig-in assignments–pulling a unit coal train through mountainous country." She adds, "What the engineers wanted most was responsiveness. Every single time they had a choice of engines (until well into the 1990s) they would choose a GM over a GE. In very recent years GE has learned lots of lessons. Not only is the company [at Erie, Pa.] the largest builder by far of diesel-electrics, but it can at last be said that General Electric makes fine locomotives. One example is the latest Dash 9 44CW with

DC traction and in the 4,300 to 4,400 horsepower range." In conclusion, it is worth noting that because diesels were not custom made and were seldom altered in any significant way, unlike most steamers, a particular model's performance on one road would be the same as on a competitor's road.

E. L. Huddleston
The Pocahontas roads gave admirers of the steam locomotive "their finest hour" right before World War II. Of the Class A, Ed King wrote, "Norfolk and Western developed the most powerful 2-6-6-4s and acquired the largest fleet, obtaining 43...between 1936 and 1950. All were equipped with cast frames and roller-bearing axles." Staufer's *C&O Power* summed up the C&O and Virginian 2-6-6-6: "Many would deny that this ultimate in Lima Super Power was ever surpassed in articulated locomotive design. The H-8 is essentially a T-1 2-10-4 slide ruled out to a 2-12-6." The 2-6-6-6 looked good from any angle, shown by 1632 rounding curve at Mt. Carbon, W. Va. in 1953.

E. L. Huddleston

H-8 no. 1600 picks up westbound loads at Thurmond, September 1955.

E. L. Huddleston

1650 in 1953, leaving Handley for run up New River to Hinton, displays interesting retrofit on side of boiler between sand domes on right side—a second turbo-generator.

The Big Three and The Number Three

The "Big Three" photo, which represents Norfolk and Western's finest road locomotive classes, excites the viewer far beyond a separate photo of each locomotive. What accounts for the impact of the three in one? Is it the camera's low angle, looking up at the subjects? Is it the associations of power that have attached to these well engineered locomotives? Or is it something else, harder to discern by ordinary measurements? Perhaps there is significance in the number three! Intrigued by the proliferation of acronyms and initialisms in American writings, I reviewed their trends in a paper for the American Name Society. One of my findings, that the most significant initialisms were in three's—like CIA, IBM, or AAA—led an attendee to recommend an essay in a sociological journal titled "The Significance of the Number Three in American Culture." Looking it up, I discovered that three's combine more often than other numerical combinations, like red, yellow, and green for traffic signals or knife, fork, and spoon for table settings. Only then did I begin to understand why a photo of three of my favorite steam locomotive types—the C&O and Virginian 2-6-6-6 Allegheny–should be so appealing, after William Ritasse, professional photographer, had them moved into position (when the sun was at the right angle) at C&O's engine terminal at Clifton Forge, Virginia, making sure Rich Patch Mountain loomed behind the the big 2-6-6-6s.

Norfolk and Western/K.L. Miller Collection

This 1943 Ritasse photo was used on the cover of *The World's Greatest Steam Locomotives* (TLC, 2001) and on the dedication page of my and Dixon's *The Allegheny, Lima's Finest* (Hundman Publishing). It was, of course, on the cover of the C&O employees magazine. N&W's "Big Three" photo (also 1943) was intended for the N&W employee magazine and for national publicity. The company photographer set up his camera at the west end of the Roanoke yards (with no mountains in view but with the necessary space). Rather than placing three of the same type of locomotives together, as Ritasse had done with the 2-6-6-6s, the photographer included the three road locomotive types with which N&W had standardized its fleet from the Depression through World War II to the end of steam. The class "J" (4-8-4) at left was used across the system on major passenger trains. The class Y-6 (and sub-classes Y-6a and Y-6b) hauled freight over the grades of the Allegheny Front, Ridge and Valley Province, and the Blue Ridge, whereas the class "A" (2-6-6-4) hauled freights exceeding a mile in length over more level divisions. In the 1940's, after the end of World War II, if one went trackside to watch N&W trains, he would mostly see these three classes on the main line and relatively few others. That would not be true on C&O. Photographer Ritasse could not have kept to his magic three, for Chessie's failure to standardize produced a much more eclectic roster of big steam locomotives. Possibly, Ritasse could have achieved a fair representation of "modern" C&O road power with four classes in the photo–a class K-4 2-8-4 for "level" division freights, the H-8 2-6-6-6 for mountain division runs, a class L-2 4-6-4 for "level" passenger runs, and a class J-3 4-8-4 for mountain passenger work. On few major American railroads could one reduce the varieties of power down to these three without being rather arbitrary in the selection. Artist Frank Reilly had tried to achieve dramatic impact with a staggered rendition of modern road power on the huge Pennsylvania Railroad for the 1946 company calendar (reproduced in Staufer's *Pennsy Power*, 1962). However, he had to use four, which reduced the impact—at left was the nose of an EMD diesel, next to it, a class T-1 4-4-4-4 Duplex steamer, then the freight Duplex class Q-2 4-4-6-4, and finally a famous GG-1 electric. The reader can make a game of this by asking, if he were the photographer, which three locomotive classes (or repetition of a single engine or 2-1 combination) he would select for a three-in-one photo of motive power on the Virginian or the Clinchfield.

Class E-1 655, sixth engine in CRR's first order for 4-6-6-4s in 1942-43, heads south with coal just south of Dante, Va., on downgrade, June 1952.

While N&W was designing its Super Power 2-6-6-4, Union Pacific was designing a Super Power 4-6-6-4. A. W. Bruce stated the 4-6-6-4 had "the best riding stability at high speeds" while the 2-6-6-4 "had riding stability at medium speeds." It all depended on what a road wanted. Well over 200 of the 4-6-6-4, type were built in the United States, and 18 of these went to the Clinchfield. At the Irwin, Tenn., coaling station July 17, 1948, is CRR 672, class E-3, former Denver & Rio Grande Western Challenger 3802, built in 1943. CRR has modified original appearance with a single smoke stack. Union Pacific influence is apparent in Elesco exhaust steam injector (above front cylinder.)

B. F. Cutler, H. H. Harwood collection

C&O K-4 (2-8-4) 2775, circa 1948, has highballed manifest train no. 92 to Elkhorn City from Russell for forwarding to the Clinchfield. The 1.5% grade through the Breaks begins at the entrance to the CRR yards. CRR 663 (4-6-6-4) assists the C&O train into the yards. CRR. 663 will then take the train to Erwin, Tenn. Shoving behind the caboose will be a CRR 4-6-6-4, 2-8-8-2, or 2-8-2 (depending on tonnage) through the Breaks to the Towers.

E. L. Huddleston

The Pocahontas roads relied on Mallets for crossing the Appalachians, but for "level-land" service in the Coastal Plain and Interior Lowlands, Mallets were "overkill." That was true for the C&O and Virginian, but not true for the N&W and Clinchfield. N&W hauled such long coal trains that even in fairly level country articulateds seemed appropriate. The CRR, to put it bluntly, had no level-land territory. C&O and Virginian, however, found good use for the Berkshire type 2-8-4 which the 2-8-2 had evolved into during the Super Power revolution of the mid-1920s. VGN 2-8-4 no. 508, copied from C&O 2-8-4, is serviced at Roanoke, Va., in 1948.

E. L. Huddleston

Lower Left: C&O 2-8-4 2707 moves 160 empties from Russell to Peach Creek in 1953 past Huntington, W.Va. C&O called its 90 2-8-4s "Kanawhas"—more appropriate than being named for the Berkshire Hills of Massachusetts! C&O donated 2707 to Cleveland in 1955; it later found permanent home at the Illinois Railway Museum. Alco RSD-5 road switcher in background—built June 1952— illustrates how in that year C&O was rapidly dieselizing, for in1952 C&O received over 112 EMD F7 and FP7 units and 26 Alco RSD-5s.

E. L. Huddleston

In the 1950s, C&O dieselized mostly with EMD products but did buy from Baldwin-Westinghouse and Alco-GE. Three years before Baldwin (which had merged with Lima-Hamilton) went out of business, C&O supplemented its existing Bladwin road switchers with two model AS-616. C&O's prior Baldwin diesels had Commonwealth cast trucks. Nos. 5528 and 5529 have tri-mount trucks, rare on Baldwins. It's July 1953 at Russell and the 5528 and 5529, brand new, are in unusual terminal-to-terminal operation to the coal fields.

General Electric U25B no. 2503 was only two months old when, in October 1963, Dr. James F. EuDaly caught 4 units at Hinton waiting for crew to go east over Alleghany Subdivision. In June 1964, this writer observed four U25Bs with coal train upgrade at Fort Spring, W. Va. From under the hood of one unit came a raucous, but methodical pounding noise, of metal on metal, suggesting literally that it had "thrown" a piston rod.

Arthur B. Johnson

Lower Left: Three "fireless" steam switchers were delivered by the H. K. Porter Co., of Pittsburgh to C&O in January, 1949, showing just how very much committed C&O's Mechanical Dept. was to steam in the seminal year of 1948. The class C-8s served for many years at Elk Yard, where they were supplied with storage steam (superheated water) for switching hazardous materials at a major Union Carbide and Carbon installation. The coupling and valve for the steam supply appear to be on top of no. 3 driver in this 1956 photo of no. 36.

E. L. Huddleston

C&O Santa Fe type (2-10-2) 4000 (ex-Wabash 2513) leaves Russell yard eastbound with freight in June 1947, as C-16 249 (0-8-0) starts to shove a long double into the eastbound yard. This switcher, built in 1943, will be sold to the Virginian Ry. in 1950, keeping its same number

E. L. Huddleston

In 1950 N&W purchased its first conventional switch engines since 1894 when it obtained second-hand from C&O practically brand new 0-8-0 switchers. N&W liked theirs so well it built at Roanoke 45 more (with larger tender and extra air pump). No. 234, working the Williamson yards in July 1953, was built that year and retired with new number in 1960.

> *"In Railroad Town the yard goats toil*
> *And powder up the rails with sand;*
> *While journals get the waste and oil,*
> *The crummy silently does stand.*
> *The hotshot's clamor fills the air;*
> *The drill crew men, all lean and brown,*
> *Go dancing nightly to the blare*
> *Of herding cars in Railroad Town."*
>
> — "In Railroad Town," by Earle F. Baker,
> quoted in Freeman Hubbard, *Railroad Avenue*

The "yard goats" that toiled in the yards deep in Appalachia have not received their due, probably because they are overshadowed by the bigger "road" freight and passenger locomotives. Even without the toiling yard engines, assembly yards were and are interesting places, especially at night, when flood lights bathed all activity in a soft glow, and warmth emanated from pot bellied stoves set under lean-to shelters between the yard "ladder" tracks. But that atmosphere is hard to reproduce on paper. Better to describe the locomotives used in yard service and its closely associated mine-run service. (Yard switching and mine run service were alike in that the men in this service worked eight-hour days rather than terminal to terminal.) Besides the types of engines used in coal assembly yards and in mine shifter service, there's the question to answer of how the coal cars that the mine runs brought into the assembly yards were actually made up into over-the-road trains.

Yard engines per se were not in widespread use on the Pocahontas roads. The Virginian had only five from the 1910 period until 1950, when it purchased second-hand from C&O 15 World War II period (1942-43) C-16 class 0-8-0s. C&O, determined to dieselize its fleet of switchers, wanted to get rid of the steamers. It is somewhat sad to know that the only Virginian steam locomotive preserved from scrapping should be one of the five 0-8-0-s dating from 1910, which were considerably lacking in boiler and firebox capacity when compared to the USRA design of 1918, on which the C&O C-16s were based. Virginian 0-8-0 no. 4 is at the Roanoke, Va., Museum of Transportation, according to Lloyd D. Lewis.

The Clinchfield, like the Virginian, never purchased switchers new for itself. Rather, in 1917 it converted two very old Consolidations to 0-8-0s, which were scrapped in 1938. Both Clinchfield and Virginian relied mostly on Mikados and Mallets for switching. What Ed King pointed out about how the N&W kept supplied with switchers (until 1949) held true for Virginian and Clinchfield also: as N&W received newer road power, it converted older power to switchers mainly by replacing road-style pilots with footboards. (Also, for engines assigned to city switching, it often added over-fire air jets to keep down black smoke.) Because Norfolk and Western amassed a fleet of 286 unusual 4-8-0, or Mastodon types, between 1906 and 1911 (and never owned any Mikados), the N&W used 2-8-0s, 4-8-0s and 2-6-6-2 and 2-8-8-2 Mallets for switching, until N&W, like the Virginian, bought C&O's most recent 0-8-0 castoffs.

Baldwin had built these 30 C-16 class switchers for C&O late in 1948. In 1949 sudden management decisions called for drastic economies of operation; among them, wholesale cuts in local and branch-line passenger trains, reducing from 25 to 10 of an order for new mine-shifter 2-6-6-2s, and ordering new Alco S-2 diesel switchers. Meanwhile, what to do with the 30 new 0-8-0 switchers, a type which had proven its worth so much in the past? Luckily, C&O's competitor, the Norfolk and Western, still wholly committed to steam, took these locomotives—at bargain prices—that in the words of Lewis Jeffries, "made up the most modern switcher fleet of its type in America." Besides mechanical lubricators and American multiple front-end throttles, these C&O C-16 rejects had the latest in smoke consumers mounted on the firebox sides and cylinders cast integrally as part of the General Steel Castings solid frame. So pleased was N&W with the efficiency and power of these workhorses that it constructed in its own Roanoke Shops 45 more of them, identical to C&O's except for modified tenders, an extra air pump, and an increase in boiler pressure from 200 to 220 lbs.

C&O had started out, like the other Pocahontas roads, using steam switchers sparingly; it had for yard and industrial switching the many Consolidations (2-8-0) of the 1900-1910 period displaced from mainline freight service by the arrival of 2-6-6-2 Mallets in large numbers. However, beginning in 1925 C&O started

Twelve-wheelers (4-8-0) were rare in America yet N&W had 286 of them. According to Ed King, N&W "kept the elderly 4-8-0s in service until 1958 because they were N&W's only freight locomotives smaller than articulateds." N&W never owned any of the most popular wheel arrangement, the Mikado (2-8-2) even though around 1912 the road asked for bids for some from the major builders. No. 383 (Alco 1906), stationed at Kenova yards, has come over to the C&O main to switch industries in 1948.

receiving 0-8-0s, built to USRA standardized dimensions, that had been introduced in 1918 when the federal government took over the railroads. The story is complex. C&O's motive power department took notice of this design through performance of the standardized switchers on the Pere Marquette Railroad, which like C&O had come under the Van Sweringen brothers' holding company umbrella around 1924. The PM had received ten original USRA 0-8-0s in 1918-1919, and C&O's subsidiary, the Hocking Valley, received ten copies in 1926. So C&O learned all about them. In 1929 C&O ordered its own copies—class C-16—but improved on the USRA design by raising boiler pressure, increasing driver diameter one inch to 52 inches and modernizing them with each order, as described above, until it owned 115 0-8-0s by 1942-43. What's so interesting about these very successful switchers is that they were basically a design of the World War I era.

Not only did C&O start buying big eight-wheeled switchers in the 1920s, it brought a sizable order of the fairly rare 0-10-0 type. Whereas according to L. D. Bruce, a total of "about 2,800" of the 0-8-0 type were built in the United States for switching service, only about "fifty or sixty" 0-10-0s were built in the United States. Interestingly, C&O liked this type so well it bought 0-10-0s before it ever ordered "modern" 0-8-0s. In January 1919, the C&O started receiving from Alco the first of an order of ten huge switchers (class

C-12) with 51-inch drivers (same diameter as the USRA 0-8-0s), their tractive effort of 62,950 lbs. being almost as much as C&O's rugged class K-2 Mikados. C&O liked them so well it bought five more in 1921.

Both C-16 eight-wheel switchers and the 0-10-0 super switchers worked the busy Peach Creek coal assembly yard from the 1920s on. An 0-8-0 worked the empty yard, and two 0-10-0 switchers worked the loaded yard. Phil Shuster, co-author of *C&O Power*, knew the C&O switcher fleet well, so his evaluation looms large: "This writer was very pleasantly surprised when, upon visiting the C&O's Peach Creek terminal in June 1956 [four months before completion of total system dieselization] he discovered two C-12s, Nos. 137 and 142, actively switching the yard there. It had been presumed that these old gals had gone to scrap years before, but there they were kicking individual hoppers of coal and doubling cuts of cars to build up a train—and smoking up all of Peach Creek in the process. It was a never-to-be-forgotten performance and that particular afternoon passed much, much too quickly."

The C-12s were replaced at Peach Creek with Alco S-2 switchers coupled together and operated as a single locomotive. By the 1980s, there was only one switcher at work, usually an EMD GP38.

Mine runs operated out of a single terminal and came back to that terminal. These numerous terminals were within the confines of the Appalachian

92   Pocahontas Switchers

E. L. Huddleston

Angling of the main steam delivery pipes gives 4-8-0 487 (Baldwin 1906) an ungainly appearance. On both N&W 383 and 457 footboards extend clear across the front ends, indicating neither is intended for the road. Yet on this July day in 1947, 457 has brought the "Kenova Turn" to Kenova and is in this view backing its train into the yard. through the wye.

Plateau Province, because all bituminous seams were in this physiographic region. And most of the terminals were located in the coal fields on the flood plains of streams–some big and some little–and usually at the confluence of streams. Let's take the period right after World War II to examine. At that time the Virginian was running shifters principally out of two terminals, Page and Mullens, W.Va. (One has to point out that sometimes Appalachian assembly yards had names independent of the communities that they were connected to. For example, Elmore was the yard at Mullens; on C&O, Elk Run Jct. was the yard at Whitesville and Cane Fork at Eskdale on Cabin Creek. For N&W there was Weller Yard at Buchanan, Va. and Auville Yard at Iaeger.) Or the yard, or terminal, might have been established by the expanding railroad in the middle of nowhere and given the name of one of the officers or trustees of the road. That was the case with Page, named for the coal mining and location engineer who served H. H. Rogers so well in expanding the Virginian into rich coal fields south of the original Deepwater Railroad. (Because the major seams have now been mined out along lower Loup Creek, Page has been abandoned as a terminal.) Then there's Sproul, named for the governor of Pennsylvania, who had invested heavily in the road up Coal River later purchased by C&O. Sproul, at the junction of the Big and Little Coal Rivers, was originally intended as the assembly yard for the Coal River field, but expansion doomed it, when yards were established farther up both Big and Little Coal. Page and Mullens are both surrounded by the high hills of the Appalachian Plateau (reminding one of the saying that the famed West Virginia hills aren't really hills;

they are valleys.) Out of these terminals ran mostly USRA styled 2-8-8-2 Mallets. The Clinchfield also depended mostly on USRA 2-8-8-2s or copies, for mine runs, based at Dante, Virginia.

On N&W, Williamson and Bluefield were points without peer as terminals combining mainline freight and passenger operations with runs up branches to coal mines and back. On these runs two types of steam engines held sway–the class Y-5 USRA heavy Mallets (2-8-8-2) and their copies, plus the "improved" USRA Mallets, class Y-6, Y-6a and Y-6b (2-8-8-2) and the class Z-1 (2-6-6-2). (I once saw a 4-8-2 on N&W's Pigeon Creek shifter working out of Williamson.)

On C&O, Peach Creek (a couple of miles north of Logan, the county seat), the busiest C&O coal assembly yard, owed its activity to the large number of seams that thickened out in Logan county and to the ease of transportation accorded by the yard and the line down the Valley being on the almost uniformly level flood plain of the Guyandotte River. For all except one big mine it was possible for loaded coal cars to move downgrade on the way to the mainline near Huntington—first down a creek and then down the Guyandotte. Practically all engines on mine runs out of Peach Creek were H-4 and H-6 2-6-6-2 Mallets. The mine shifters often were named–names recognizable at the Peach Creek yard office by crew caller, yard master, and car distributor, and by yard crews and car "knockers' who worked the mine shifters. For example, two that Bob Harvey recalled were the "Merry Widow" and the "Hummer." These shifters brought coal cars directly from the coal mines to the terminal where they were switched by 0-8-0 switchers (in the empty yard) and 0-10-0 switchers in the loaded yard. Coal cars came into the yard unsorted by direction. The chief responsibility for the "mine run" crew was not to bring a "no bill" into Peach Creek, for a car without a bill (identified at this point by an accompanying mine tag) was a lost car. If there was a problem with a loaded car, it was shunted into the "holder" track. Likewise, if the car inspectors found a car defective (usually in its running or draft gear) it was shoved into a track for shops.

The initial job of switching required only that the cars be blocked for the scales at which they would be weighed and officially billed. (This was of course before the use of main line scales that could weigh each car in the train as it passed over the scales at about five mph.) Making sure each mine tag was lined up with the position of the car in the incoming train, the yard clerk at Peach Creek would mark for the yardmaster the switching designations, which were "eastbound," "westbound" (using shorthand "CD" for Cincinnati Division) , and "short loads." (This writer assumes there might have been additional switching designations for "Tidewater" cars bound for freighters at Newport News that were under "rush" orders or for differentiating short loads as to cars intended for set-off at Huntington or Ceredo-Kenova for river transfer.) Cars for rail to river transfer at Huntington were put on the head-end of a "CD" if they exceeded in number what the "bulldog" between Peach Creek and Huntington was able to handle daily.

The runs from Peach Creek east to Handley (main line terminal about 110 miles away) and west to Russell (about 95 miles) were handled by 2-8-4s and 2-8-2s mostly from end of World War II until dieselization. Train length on the "mine runs" was usually 40 to 80 cars, depending on the size of the mine served and the number of mines switched on a single run of eight hours. Length of trains going toward the main-line east and west was up to 144 cars, officially 11,500 tons for the K-4 2-8-4s. (The tonnage was estimated based on capacity of car; the train would not be weighed until each car passed over the scale while moving at the Russell "hump." Trains headed east would be shoved as cuts over scales at Clifton Forge.) These terminal-to-terminal runs were paid on the basis of eight hours as a day (maximum hours of service was then 16) and 100 miles as a division.

The C&O, at the end of World War II, had numerous assembly yards. Besides Peach Creek, similar but smaller scale operations were at six additional locations in West Virginia (two of them noted above), three in Kentucky, and one in Ohio. Most of N&W's highly productive mines were located within a confined area geographically, making for more efficiency in assembling the coal cars. Its biggest assembly yard, not far as the crow flies from Peach Creek, was at Williamson. Unlike Peach Creek, Williamson was on the N&W main line. This meant all westbound coal

passed through the terminal, besides the coal coming into the yard from branch lines in the area. There was precious little yard space in Williamson, on the flood plain of Tug Fork, for switching to take place. For this reason, N&W required its mine shifter crews to do more than merely couple up the billed loads under the tipple tracks. (At that time mines loaded several grades of coal which required separate tracks for each screening.)

Because at Williamson there was not room for a separate loaded and empty yard, as there was along the flood plain at Peach Creek, N&W had precious little room for flat switching required to block the loaded cars into train-length cuts to be billed at Williamson (set-offs for Kenova), those sent west (the majority) to Portsmouth, and east to Roanoke (that included the Tidewater classification) , and eastbound cars for billing at Bluefield. To reduce the amount of switching done at Williamson, N&W switched the loaded coal cars under the tipple before bringing them into Williamson. Doing so required the mine-run conductor to be a yard clerk and yardmaster combined. To cut down on the paper work initially required at the mine head, N&W devalued the "mine tag" (which specified lading, consignor, consignee, and sometimes route) separately accompanying each car and relied on color coding "tacked" onto the car itself, specifically on the "route card board" (C&O's designation for the wooden placard on the car's lower left side). An account by Henry B. Comstock in *Railroad* (February 1944) clarifies the procedure: "Each colliery has its own miniature yard, you might say, with receiving, loading, and outbound trackage. Generally, it's a gravity layout, so that empties can be coasted under the tipples and then on into the clear. During the return trip, the engine hauls out the loads, or rather, such of them as have been tagged by the shipper, and switches them into cuts, according to the color of the tag. We use blue and white for cars consigned to Williamson scales, green for Portsmouth, orange for Bluefield, and white for Roanoke." (Comstock here quotes directly assistant car-distributor Frank Alexander interviewed in his "phone-cluttered cubicle on the third floor of the main yard-office" as he distributes "a thousand cars a day to the more than 50 mines in the Williamson area.")

Only once did I observe this switching technique. Late in 1958 my brother and I drove up the Lenore Branch (also known as the Pigeon Creek branch, location of O. Winston Link's recording "Second Pigeon and the Mockingbird"). This short December day we found the shifter, powered by class Y6 2138, four miles beyond Delbarton, just east of Ragland. No. 2138 was working forward and back in long movements on a "lead," not connected to numbered yard tracks but to tracks under the tipple, which was out of sight around a curve up beyond where we were standing. During the hour or so we were there the

C&O C-16 185 (Alco 1930) works the Peach Creek empty yard in April 1954 while Mallet compound 1494 (Alco 1920) waits to couple onto train. The 2-6-6-2 mine shifter will serve an unknown number of the 48 or so active mines in the field today.

shifter, working in simple because of the heavy gradient produced by the fall of the creek, blasted forward, paused, backed downgrade, paused again, then pushed forward again. How commands for the movements were given was unknown to us, for locomotive cabs at this time were not equipped with radios and no switchman giving hand signals was in view up the tracks. The switching was time consuming because, for safety's sake, air was kept in the cars at all times, requiring the coupling and uncoupling of air hoses and opening and closing of angle cocks on every move.

At Danville, W.Va., 2-8-0 no. 1037 (built 1909) is ready for run to mine at Monclo (Boone County Coal Corp.). Engineer stands in gangway. 1037 will back up to mine with caboose and one box car. It will pull 50 or more loads. 2-6-6-2 Mallet will supply the mine with empties at night.

E. L. Huddleston

C&O C-16 192 waits on the lead to the Peach Creek empty yard in 1954 for a hand signal to move forward as 0-10-0 137 starts backing in order to kick some cars into the loaded yard. Both switch engines are peppy with sharp exhausts, and they put on quite a show for the railfan photographer.

E. L. Huddleston

Suddenly 0-8-0 192 blasts forward as 0-10-0 137 overcomes the inertia of the loaded coal cars. C&O 2-8-4s will take the loads, arranged into trains of 140 to 144 cars, to either Russell or Handley.

E. L. Huddleston

In his history of the steam locomotive Alfred Bruce of Alco had few good things to say about the never very popular 0-10-0 type. Yet this 1919 locomotive in 1956, looked good and sounded good in heavy duty switching at Peach Creek, which is what it had done steadily from the booming 1920s, through Depression and war. There was no doubt this Alco (Richmond) product was the heaviest and most powerful of its type. With the same basic lines as the famous C-16 0-8-0, it has a much bigger boiler and fire box.

from storage into the coal cars (now mostly having "bath tub" bottoms instead of hopper-bottoms for ease in dumping) at a steady rate sufficient to fill each car to uniform height while the cars move forward under the load-out, powered by the shifter's locomotives (which are apt to be identical to over-the-road units in assignment). The flow of slack-grade coal through a single chute is so regulated that it stops after filling each car, and picks up with the next, without requiring the train to stop.

With evolving changes in coal preparation technology and in the gradual narrowing of markets into metallurgical and steam coals, the procedure followed by a shifter today differs from procedures described above, which were common some forty years ago. The structure at which now, typically, loading takes place is called a "load-out," not a "tipple." At a load-out a technologically sophisticated operation takes place, for coal of uniform sizing is "metered"

This procedure, aptly called "flood loading," requires that the cars move at a uniform pace under the loader. To assure uniformity, the cab of the lead locomotive is equipped with a speed-control device–on CSX patented as the "Pace Setter" or "Speed Control II." This device has to perform quite a job, keeping the train moving at a uniform pace, typically under a half-mile an hour, despite changes in resistance caused by curves, shifts in gradient, or increases in tonnage accumulating behind the locomotives.

Once continuous loading is completed—a process that can take several hours depending on the length of the train to be loaded–the mine shifter returns its

E. L. Huddleston

Ten-wheel switcher no. 142, seen in 1954, spent its entire life at Peach Creek, just like 137, and the same shop force worked on both. Yet study of detail reveals differences. One real alteration is the differing design of the step on the pilot beam permitting access to the running board.

loads, with little chance of a "no-bill" occurring–to the assembly yard. Some really big mines, most of these being surface mines, load enough cars in one run that the cut from the mine automatically assumes the status of an over-the-road train and therefore bypasses handling (but not a crew change) at the assembly yard. Another big difference from the procedures followed at mid-century is in-motion weighing, where coal moving out of the assembly yards is weighed at one location (if headed in one direction), usually on a main line, where track is level and where speed can be slowed to approximately five mph while the train moves over the scales. The scales are usually located so that there need be only one for westbounds and one for eastbounds, even though the train might have originated at one of several coal field terminals.

E. L. Huddleston
For flat switching loaded coal cars, the C&O 0-10-0 had few peers in making "snappy" movements. A 2-6-6-2 Mallet could (and did) do this type switching, but its movements would be slower and coal consumption greater. C&O 0-10-0 No. 137 in June 1956 works lead in front of yard office. Crew of 0-8-0, at right, takes "spot" while yard conductor gets orders from Peach Creek yard master.

E. L. Huddleston

In October 1949, C&O 2734 brings 140 cars down Little Coal toward the main line at St. Albans. Here at Sproul, named for governor of Pennsylvania who was in investment syndicate that later sold out to C&O, is junction of Big Coal branch (foreground). Confluence of Big and Little Coal Rivers is about 2 miles down the line. This was to have been a town (with C&O officials having insider real estate knowledge) until decision for a bigger terminal upstream near Madison.

E. L. Huddleston
C&O's most concentrated and productive coal field was the Logan County, yet its assembly yard was located 65 winding miles up the Guyandotte river from the main line junction at Barboursville. All ten of the 1949 order for Mallet compound 2-6-6-2s went in service at Peach Creek, including 1306, preparing to leave the empty yard for a mine run assignment.

E. L. Huddleston

By 1950, with the exception of Nelsonville, Ohio, Cane Fork, West Virginia, was C&O's smallest mine assembly terminal. Located ten miles up Cabin Creek from the main line, Cane Fork had a large engine house (seen above 2-6-6-2 1451), a coal and sand tower (at left) a yard office (at right) a scale leading to a coal classification yard, and a signal directing movements to that yard.

Roger Whitt

In contrast to C&O's 50-ton capacity coaling station at Cane Fork is the 1200-ton capacity coaling station of the N&W at Williamson, West Virginia, illustrating the concentration of mine run activities on N&W, together with main line runs. Unique feature of this structure is a cable car (visible at upper right) that conveys coal from a drift mine located on hillside across the Tug Fork to the coaling station's storage bins. Whether in 1958 the conveyor still operates is uncertain, for a string of loaded coal cars awaits unloading at right. Engines visible are 2-6-6-4s, awaiting calls for runs to Portsmouth, Ohio.

Bluefield, West Virginia, was not so busy in1952 as base for mine runs, mainly because there were no mines east of the Bluestone branch (which was in decline) and because of change in land forms from Appalachian Plateau to Ridge and Valley. However, there are 7 Mallets visible in this view. Some are main line pusher engines and the one with men on the pilot is a yard switcher. Dreary YMCA building overlooks the smoky scene, and near right edge of the picture are big smoke ducts that are supposed to reduce emissions.

E. L. Huddleston
Where Dry Fork emptied into Tug Fork across the river from Iaeger, W.Va., was Weller Yard, a branch line terminal. But there was hardly a busier one as long as Pocahontas No. 3 seam was being mined. There was not room for a turntable in the narrow bottoms, but a wye for turning connected the branch to the main line. In this 1957 view, there are still manifold mine shifters based here.

Gary E. Huddleston

Top: On a snowy December 1958, a few miles up Dry Fork from Iaeger, mine shifter engine 2176 backs up while switching a coal mine located along the stream. All class Y-6b Mallets, like this one, were assigned in a pool to both main line and branch line service.

Left: 2176 now brings its train toward Iaeger on same 1958 day. Shifter will soon enter tunnel. The few empty hoppers on head end are probably cars that the mine or mines served have rejected for loading. Backing up was a common direction for mine shifters.

Gary E. Huddleston

Left: Another shifter heads toward Iaeger, with still another long cut of coal off Dry Creek branch. Engineer of 2-8-8-2 Mallet 2122 does not see a need to shift his position while backing down the twisting line.

Bottom: Moving back and forth on the lead to the big coal preparation plant (out of sight at right) of the Island Creek Coal Co. at Delbarton is everyday activity for 2-8-8-2s like Y-6 2138. The N&W Mallet is switching cars into cuts according to their scale destination, designated by color of card stapled to lower left end of car. When all billed loads are pulled, 2138 will head 15 miles down Pigeon Creek to junction at Naugatuck and on to Williamson.

E. L. Huddleston

Top Right: Not all N&W mine shifters were 2-6-6-2s or 2-8-8-2s. Heavy Mountain type 103, built in the Company Shops in 1916, waits on the Lenore Branch near Naugatuck, for an unknown reason, before proceeding to Delbarton in 1957. Though built in Roanoke, the 4-8-2 is equipped with the Hodges type trailing truck, developed at Baldwin Locomotive Works in Philadelphia. N&W's other Mountain types had either the Cole-Scoville type (from Alco) or the Delta type (developed in 1920s).

E. L. Huddleston

A C&O mine shifter, pulled by an H-6 2-6-6-2, heads toward Thurmond from mine at Garden Ground in June 1950. The structures visible at Price Hill Jct. (near Mt. Hope, WV) are all standard C&O design: from the privy at left and the section foreman's dwelling in center, to the motor car shed and operator's shack at right.

Everett N. Young

Statistics tell the story. In 1950 C&O owned 60,000 gondola and hopper cars, N&W owned 47,000, Virginian 15,000, and Clinchfield (or CC&O) 6,000. Yet mines on the CRR—Moss, Va., comes first to mind—could be just as large as any on the other three roads. This preparation plant at Trammel, Va., near the north portal of Sandy Ridge Tunnel, is on the edge of the Appalachian Plateau and is a relatively small operation. Date is October, 1975, and coal train led by SD40 heads south.

Peg Dobbin for Fairbanks-Morse, H. H. Harwood Collection

The Virginian Railway, starting in 1954, dieselized its coal field operations with 2400 H.P. diesels from Fairbanks-Morse in Beloit, Wisconsin. Instead of a "V-16" engine like GM used, these had 24 opposed pistons in an in-line block of twelve. The Navy used these engines successfully on submarines in World War II, but when applied to rugged railroad service, their maintenance presented a problem, especially coupling the two crank shafts. Called "Trainmasters," these attractive diesels fit in well with the landscape near Helen, W.Va. on Virginian's Winding Gulf branch. C&O's competing line through the Winding Gulf field is in foreground.

Peg Dobbin for Fairbanks-Morse, Herb Harwood Collection

Top Left and Above: The Fairbanks-Morse company photographer, in 1955, discovered that the most scenic spot in the Virginian coal fields was the loop in the Winding Gulf field climbing from the Guyandotte basin to the plateau surrounding Beckley, W.Va. After depositing Peg Dobbin at one end of the loop, the crew backed to the tunnel and then proceeded around the loop, permitting a sequence of photos. C&O's competing line in the "Gulf," passing under the Virginian bridge, ascends to plateau level by means of a switchback.

Gary E. Huddleston

Bottom Left: Perspective of the Winding Gulf loop as seen from C&O tracks. Peg Dobbin would have been standing just around curve from front of Virginian Trainmaster heading back to Mullens in June 1959.

Charles Clegg, California State Railroad Museum Collection

Near Schuyler, in historic Albemarle County and amid the distinctly rural scenery of the Virginia Piedmont, 2-6-2T no. 9 of the N&A heads toward Warren in January, 1946.

Mainline railroading might be defined as a stretch of track on which there are both named passenger trains and scheduled through freights (as opposed to extras and way freights). C&O and N&W had mainlines that met this criterion. The Virginian and Clinchfield met it only halfway--by having scheduled through freight trains but no through passenger trains, only "locals." (Although coal trains were mostly run as extras, it was the solid coal trains-- and the empties-- that gave the traffic density which was such an appealing part of the Pocahontas region carriers.) So perhaps any one of these factors present on a line would define mainline railroading.

But there was an appeal of railroading in Appalachia which was almost opposite the appeal of mainline railroading. That was the appeal of independent short lines that conducted their business in unhurried and informal ways and usually with second-hand equipment. Some of these carriers were not even standard gauge, and some were not independent, in that they were affiliated with an industry, like a coal or lumber company. Although some were quite functional, their appeal was usually not in their capability and adaptability to demands of the present. Rather, it was their stubbornly holding onto a style of operation and a way of conducting business that had gone largely unchanged for perhaps fifty years.

This mode of operation probably hung on longer in Appalachia than in any other part of the country, except for the Deep South, as a look in Beebe and Clegg's *Mixed Train Daily* substantiates. That title, by the way, suggests one of the most appealing characteristics of a great many of such short lines, and that is passenger service conducted by tacking an old "combine" coach to the rear end of the road's way freight and substituting it for a caboose. Another book title that by its wording seems to sum up the appeal of such short lines is *Slow Train to Yesterday* by Archie Robinson.

By satellite I mean a short line that connected with one of the four roads (and maybe with a nearby competitor) and was dependent on one or both these connections for an economic lifeline. The name of the road did not mean a lot but sometimes added to the picturesqueness. For example, there was the seven-mile long Kanawha "Central" and the twenty-six mile long Kanawha, Glen Jean, and "Eastern" and the vague Chesapeake "Western." Some had nicknames, like "Tweetsie" for the East Tennessee and Western North Carolina. Some achieved fame by coverage in books, and some are hard to find even in old copies of the Official Guide, like the Black Mountain. Some were absorbed by the chief road they were the satellite of and became branch lines. Because the branches lacked the independent identity of a "satellite" road, they don't have quite the same appeal, yet they could create a lot of interest. Receiving acclaim were two branches of the Norfolk and Western. The Blacksburg Branch, on which ran a mixed train nicknamed "Huckleberry," had started life in 1902 (as Bill Warden states) "as part of Virginia Anthracite Coal & Railway Company." Students at Virginia Tech used this train "when traveling between their homes and school at Vacation periods" (Richard Prince). The 56-mile Abingdon Branch, whose mixed train was called the "Virginia Creeper," passed within sight of Mt.

Wally Johnson
Pulled by. no. 9, February 4, 1950, the N&A mixed train has arrived at Warren, Va., junction with C&O's James River line, and prepares to leave a "cut" for C&O to pick up. C&O's Warren depot is barely visible in background.

Rogers, highest in Virginia, and was once the independent Virginia-Carolina Railroad.

One satellite road that combined the best of an independent short line and a picturesque branch line was the Nelson and Albemarle, which was independent for eighteen miles from Rockfish to Esmont, Va., and which from Esmont to Warren, six miles, had trackage rights over the C&O's Alberene Sub-division. Both Lucius Beebe and Archie Robinson treat the N&A prominently. Beebe, in 1947, wrote:

> "The Nelson and Albemarle Railway, the property of the Albemarle Stone Corporation, is probably unique in that it is the only railroad known to the authors which at once runs regularly scheduled daily passenger trains and whose motive-power roster consists entirely of saddle-tank locomotives. The N. & A. is the last word in backwoods railroading. Its province...is a particularly remote and inaccessible domain of quarries and forests in the deep heart of the Blue Ridge Mountains [foothills, actually], and its three tiny, low-wheeled engines pant urgently through an astonishing countryside to connect with the Chesapeake and Ohio [at Esmont] and the Southern [at Rockfish] and ferry out its parent company's products from the steep quarries at Schuyler, Virginia. Schuyler, Esmont and Warren are in Albemarle County with its Thomas Jefferson associations and lie, roughly, thirty miles south of Charlottesville."

Beebe did not live long enough to know that this countryside would be the setting of "Walton's Mountain" and that "John Boy" Walton (as created by Earle Hamner, Jr.) would claim a fictionalized Schuyler, Va, as his birthplace and mountain home on his TV series.

Beebe is at his descriptive best in giving a word picture of the little train headed by a 2-6-2 saddle-tanker, which never turns: "The right of way crosses and recrosses the highway and the little train, usually consisting of three or four high cars, a couple of empty coal gondolas and the borrowed [C&O combine no. 411] coach, is a pretty thing to see, winding down its woodland path with all the dumpy dignity of Queen Victoria negotiating a particularly difficult staircase." Beebe continues: "After lunch [at Esmont] it rolls bravely on to meet the C&O's James River Division at Warren, retracing its route, coal bunker foremost, to Esmont and Schuyler late in the afternoon...Basically a utilitarian railroad and plain as an old shoe, the Nelson and Albemarle wears its borrowed coach with an air of elegance, an assurance that, like the rich Southern, or for that matter the haughty and far-off New York Central, it too can boast a passenger or two when it is so minded. The time may yet come when antiquarians and railroad aficionados will beat a path over the winding roads of the Blue Ridge to ride the clattering coach with Conductor Drumheller."

Archie Robinson had described the same run some two years before in his pioneering *Slow Train to Yesterday*. One senses that Beebe was competing

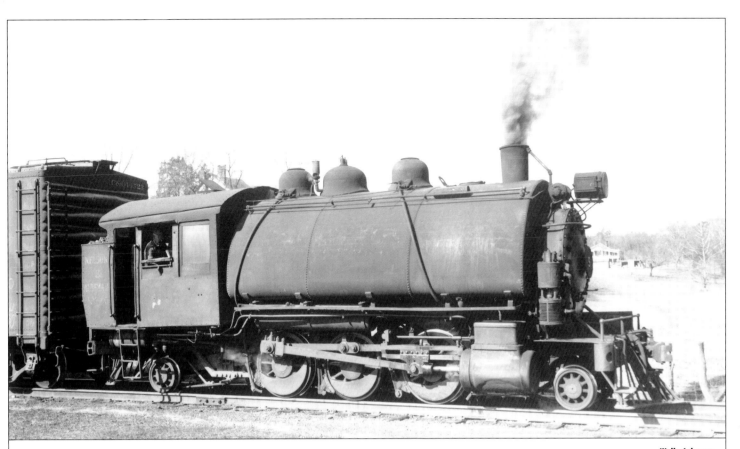

Posed at the end of its run at Warren, February 1950, no. 9 will soon be retired from service. There's a "cow catcher" on both ends and the road's name is barely visible on side of coal bunker.

with Robinson to see who could give the best account of the short ride. Both accumulate fascinating detail, both tell about the Hollywood movie shot near there in late 1940, both repeat the same anecdote about a closed bank, both ride the line and both interview the crew. From Robinson one does learn that the little train made twelve miles per hour through the scenic countryside, and one gets a detailed description of the engine, perhaps because Robinson provides no photos. (Beebe's companion. Charles Clegg, provided an excellent shot of 2-6-2T no. 9 ambling through the woods with the C&O combine, a coal car, and box car.) From his description we learn that no. 9 "has a headlight and cowcatcher at both ends" and that the water tank slung over the boiler looks "like saddle-bags on a horse." No. 9 was built new in the 1920s, and in 1951 was replaced by a General electric 44-ton diesel.

A fascinating part of the history of the N&A is its being selected to provide "on location" settings for a Hollywood movie. Both Robinson and Beebe cover the story, but there are differing details in both, including neither getting the title exactly right. *Virginia*, as reviewed in the New York Times. January 29, 1941, starring Madeleine Carroll, Fred MacMurray, and Sterling Hayden, relives the resentment of "rebels" for Yankees at the end of the Civil War. But the reviewer feels the romantic interest in the film "smacks too much of magnolias and moonshine to be

convincing." On the positive side, *Virginia* "does contain some lovely color shots of the beautiful Piedmont country of Virginia–the red earth and green-dressed fields and the Blue Ridge Mountains in the distance. These, at least, help to carry one back." This is where the N&A comes in. Both Robinson and Beebe agreed that "it was planned to use the Esmont station as the prototype of all rustic depots and Miss Carroll was slated to step down from a period-design coach while cameras ground." (As Robinson put it, the producers "rightly decided there was no station more rural than Esmont.") But at the last moment the director backed out. As to why, the two writers disagree. Beebe said they decided to go to a studio sound stage to film the scene. Robinson said the Esmont location was too shady. I agree with his account, for I saw this film as a ten-year-old and recall that a school mate with relatives in south central Virginia said it was shot at a C&O depot. Robinson said that after the Esmont location was rejected, "The N. & A.'s train moved out to the main line [at Warren] of the Chesapeake & Ohio, with a C&O crew aboard." All I can remember about the station scene was that the train that arrived was a "doodle-bug" (gas-electric motor coach). So maybe they went down to Warren, junction with the C&O's James River line, where a gas-electric motor car was used on the James river local. On the other hand, the filming could have been on the N&A, because according to the Chesapeake

E. L. Huddleston

The "little train," whose passage from the the scene was lamented by a 'little old lady," returned as tourist train Tweetsie, on new narrow-gauge trackage north of Blowing Rock, North Carolina. The engine, no. 12, a 4-6-0 built by Baldwin for the ET&WNC in 1917, performs in public in the summer of 1957. According to Bob Harvey, no. 12 "had two or three changes of ownership and location after the ET&WNC was abandoned. At one time Gene Autry had it. Then the Shenandoah Central got it and had it running for a while." Finally, "Grover Robbins of Boone bought the engine and cars and had the railroad built near Blowing Rock."

and Ohio Historical Society, "a motor car was used on some passenger runs." D. Wallace Johnson, authority on steam railroading in Virginia in this period, says that the shooting location finally chosen was the hamlet of Howardsville, five and a half miles west of Warren on the C&O's James River freight line, about 91 miles west of Richmond in the Piedmont.

An article on Virginia short lines in the *Bulletin* of the National Railroad Historical Society included the N & A, but that was after the line was abandoned in 1963. The N&A and the Alberene Railroad were completed in 1898; C&O bought the latter in 1902. In 1948 the connection with the Southern was severed by a washout of a bridge between Rockfish and Schuyler. In February 1950 passenger service ended when coach 411 was removed from the former mixed train consist. The Old Dominion Railroad Club of Richmond sponsored a fan trip on the last passenger run. The trip "proved to be one of the best in the history of the club," according to the Club's bulletin.

(The crew was the same as had accompanied Beebe and Clegg's ride, as well as Archie Robinson's.) Lewis D. Rubin, Jr., distinguished scholar of American literature at the University of North Carolina, was on this last run. And his *A Memory of Trains* (2000) accumulates details to add to the accounts of train riding on the N&A by Beebe and Robinson: "The passenger coach, a combine which also housed the baggage compartment, had green plush seats, oil lamps, and a pot bellied stove.... . The right-of-way led past old quarries, high cuts, hills and rolling fields, with the tracks groaning and swaying on the cross ties as the train steamed by.... ."

With there being so much "romance" associated with this C&O satellite, I decided in the late 1980's, when in the vicinity, to drive to Warren and see if I could picture what the junction had been like when Robinson described his arrival there behind no. 9: I had topographical maps with me, but found the winding one-lane, paved roads confusing. There were no roads along the flood plain of the James that permitted driving directly from Scottsville (a place John Boy Walton sometimes mentioned) to Warren. The Piedmont countryside was lonely. The only person I encountered was an elderly farmer out looking for his wife, who had wandered away. When I got on a road that led to the tracks, I could see that Warren was no longer a place. There was a clearing there; that was all you could say for it. The James River Sub-Division track was heavily ballasted and of welded rail, with no trace of a siding or a turnout to the former N&A connection. There was no trace of the depot or other building, and one even had difficulty determining the right-of-way of the N&A as it took off in a northwesterly direction. This isolation was in contrast with what Archie Robinson found when he rode the train down to Warren in the early 1940s: "At a siding a few yards from the tracks of the C. & O.'s James River Division we halted, and I went up to photograph the engine, an object of genuine interest. No. 9 is a small, plump locomotive...A two-car local of the C. & O. halted on the main line in front of C. W. Whitted's country store, and the station agent trundled the mail-sack across to the waiting N. & A. Inside the store it was cool, dark, and appetizing...Having left a couple of cars of soapstone and one of slate on a siding for the next C&O way freight, Number 9 blew for the backward run [from Warren] through Esmont to Schuyler, which is headquarters of the line. Mr. Drumheller, the conductor...offered a drink [of warm water] from a quart bottle."

Another satellite associated with a Pocahontas road which has achieved a permanent place in railroad folklore is the narrow-gauge East Tennessee and Western North Carolina, known as Tweetsie since the 1930's, its name conferred by boys and girls attending summer camp at Banner Elk (on the line) in the Blue Ridge. Today Blue Ridge Parkway tourists know of the Tweetsie as a two-mile, oval tracked, narrow-gauge attraction located near Blowing Rock, eight miles from Boone, North Carolina, which used to be the eastern terminus of the real road. For years Baldwin- built (1917) no. 12, one of the ET&WNC's Ten-Wheeler locomotives, headed the tourist train. Both Archie Robinson, native of the area, and Lucius Beebe, visitor, devote plenty of space to the real thing.

A capsule history appears in the *Historical Guide to North American Railroads*. Opened as a narrow-gauge in 1882 between Johnson City, Tennessee, and Cranberry, North Carolina, the road added the Linville Railroad in 1913, giving it an additional 33 miles to Boone. In the Depression the ET&WNC turned to tourism to fill its trains. The 1941 floods caused the Linville portion to be abandoned. In 1950 the narrow gauge portion east of Elizabethton was abandoned. (Between Elizabethton and Johnson City, with connections to the Clinchfield and Southern,

the ET&WNC had since 1906 installed rails for both standard and narrow-gauge service.) In World War II a rayon plant was built at Elizabethton , which gave new life to the last segment of the ET&WNC. The real Tweetsie lived up to its reputation as a railfan's delight by using ex-Southern Consolidations nos. 207 and 208 until 1967, when a pair of Alco road switchers from the Southern replaced them. Nos. 207 and 208 (after renumbering) ended up at the Tennessee Valley Railroad Museum at Chattanooga.

Just as he had done for the Nelson and Albemarle, Lucius Beebe was able to bring to bear his "down East" sophistication as a writer on the ET&WNC, yet he was awake to the "wonderful and beautiful upland" surrounding the ET&WNC, and the independence of the native western Carolinians living in the Grandfather mountain country: "Tweetsie itself is a rare, dainty and proud narrow gauge. Its locomotives are Swiss-watch anachronisms with red- and gold-capped stacks, red-painted cab window frames and rod assemblies that might have come from a jeweler's display window. When we visited it, the head-end crew of No. 12 had caught and were maintaining in the tool box of their locomotive a large and understandably ungracious possum [which the crew took to Johnson City]. In cabins along the right of way at Cranberry and Roan Mountain aged beldames in men's felt hats stood in the doors of unpainted but spotless cabins to watch the train pass." Once again, Beebe seemed to be trying to outdo Archie Robinson's description of the same train and engine: "[At Boone], Robinson wrote, " panting from her run up the mountain, stood the shortest, slimmest train I had ever seen. On the three-foot track was a single car carved in ...slices: United States Mail, express, and passengers...It was coupled to a ten-wheel steam engine with a slender smokestack and a flaring cow-catcher. In the glow from the fire-box green paint shone on the lettering...The driving -wheels were painted red, as in a Currier and Ives print." (The triple combine is on display today at the North Carolina Transportation Museum at Spencer, N.C.)

This survey of picturesque satellites of the four Pocahontas roads might continue if space allowed. I can think of three others with a long history and a close following that I feel a little guilty in not pursuing, for I have followed them for a long time--the Meadow River Lumber Company, which ran over NF&G (jointly owned by C&O and NYC from Rainelle to its own temporary tracks high in the mountains), the Winifrede Railroad in West Virginia and the Morehead and North Fork in Kentucky. For all the reader wants to know about the M&NF up to about the mid-1940s, he can go to *Ghost Railroads of Kentucky* (reprinted 1998 by Indiana University Press) for an article first published in the *Kentucky Engineer* at the University of Kentucky where author Elmer Sulzer was a Communications Professor. From

E. L. Huddleston

As far back as 1906 the ET&WNC had installed a third rail for standard gauge traffic between Johnson City and Elizabethton, Tennessee, and this trackage remained in service after abandonment of the narrow gauge in 1950. Here, at Elizabethton, ex-Southern no. 207, built by Alco in 1904, is on "spot" in summer of 1957 in revenue service. 207 served with 208 (both featuring Southern type valve gear) until 1967, when, according to George Drury, they were replaced with a pair of Alco road-switchers from the Southern Ry. Southern took them back for excursion service.

right after World War II until the 1960s, one could go to Clearfield, Ky., a few miles from Morehead, and see three well kept steam locomotives, which alternated in service monthly in bringing down from Clack Mountain fire clay (in second-hand ore cars mostly) for preparation in the kilns of the Lee Clay Products Co. as drain tiles and other products. Occasionally the M&NF's locomotive would wander a mile or so over to the junction with the C&O's Lexington Division to pick up or leave a coal car. The brick company seemed to do a lot of business, but its products were shipped out by trucks to Pennsylvania, the company apparently uncertain the railroads could handle the shipments without damaging them.

The three locomotives were Prairie type (2-6-2) no. 11, 0-6-0 switcher no. 12, and 0-6-0 no. 14, all serviced at a shop maintained by the M&NF. No. 11 was the most interesting partly because by the 1950's the Prairie was not a type one often saw. The type was first built for the Lake Shore and Michigan Southern

in 1901 and was intended as a heavy express-train engine. The perky looking 2-6-2 of the M&NF was built for the Kanawha, Glen Jean and Eastern in 1909. With driver diameter of only 48 inches, it was obviously not intended for express-train service! The KGJ&E was one of those very interesting Appalachian coal-carrying short lines which went out of business when the C&O absorbed it in the 1940s. (As of year 2000 the high smoke stacks of its locomotive shops were still standing at Carlyle, near Mt. Hope, W.Va.) KGJ&E no. 200 was on its way to scrapping, when M&NF officials got word that it was passing through Russell, Ky., where they inspected it and bought it, presumably at scrap price. After leaving the M&NF, no. 11 (nee 200) served in excursion service from 1965 to 1970 on the Everett Railroad in Pennsylvania. Today it is stored at Williams Grove Amusement Park, west of Everett. No. 12 (0-6-0) was built in 1905 as no. 1643 for the giant Southern Ry., and spent most of its life before the M&NF acquired

Gary E. Huddleston

By the time Elmer Sulzer wrote *Ghost Railroads of Kentucky*, practically all the old roads were "gone with the wind." One, however, with a proud awareness of its function as an Appalachian short line, kept going into the 1960s. This was the Morehead and North Fork, which connected with C&O near Morehead, Ky., in the hills of the Cumberland Plateau. No. 11, a 2-6-2, or Prairie type, blows its whistle in front of the well kept headquarters of the road at Clearfield, Ky., in 1958.

it in 1952 working as a local switcher at Princeton, Indiana. Today it is stored at Clearfield. No. 14 was built in 1944 for the Union Railroad as no. 77. the M&NF acquired it in 1955. In 1969 it went to the Cumberland Falls Scenic Railway at Parkers Lake, Ky.

The M&NF had such a devoted following that people who had read about it or had visited Clearfield started wondering if it could be made into a tourist road. (The four mile run from Clearfield to the mines was up a scenic hollow and was about the right length for a pleasurable train trip.) After the steamers were retired early in the 1960s, the road dieselized with second hand Alcos. When the M&NF changed hands, the new owner acquired three former Durham & Southern Baldwin RS12's to replace the Alcos. Then the whole operation went belly up. For what has happened to the M&NF since then, one needs communicate with the M&NF's historian and chief promoter, James Johnson of Clearfield. In a 1999 letter, Mr. Johnson wrote: "Several of us tried very hard to bring the railroad back to life from 1991

to 1996. These efforts include: bringing ex-Durham and Southern Baldwin RS-12 (1200) back to operating condition; moving old number 12 [ex-Southern 0-6-0] to a drier and safer place (for now); giving #12 a cosmetic restoration and mechanical evaluation for operation; moving in a B&O caboose from Lexington [Ky.]; moving in a 12-ton Plymouth [diesel] locomotive from London [Ky.]; having two display weekends in 1993 and 1994; putting in 300 ties by hand; restoring motor car equipment; and the list goes on."

And lest we forget, there was the six-mile long Kanawha Central Railway that operated about as long as the M&NF and that was even more remotely tucked away in the hills of Appalachia.

E. L. Huddleston
Ex-Southern no. 12 spent much of its life working at Princeton, Indiana, before M&NF acquired it. In this 1959 view, the boiler is kept polished with "waste" and M&NF's only box car is parked in front of the engine house.

Gary Huddleston
Flat lighting on the polished locomotive (in Sept. 1958) makes possible study of detail including frame, spring rigging, and main rod construction. This 2-6-2 had a privileged career, first among the coal rich hills surrounding Glen Jean and Mt. Hope, W.Va., and then in the Cumberlands of eastern Kentucky.

Both: Gary E. Huddleston

Right: Well kept no. 12, ex-Southern Ry. 0-6-0, brings cars of clay down grade to the brick works at Clearfield in 1958.

Bottom: M&NF no. 12 backs up the grade with empty clay cars, many of which are used iron ore cars.

E. L. Huddleston

At Winifrede, W.Va., seven miles up Fields Creek, Consolidation no. 8 is ready to go to work on the Winifrede Railroad, in business since 1854. No. 8, built for the C&O and in the 1920s numbered 968, will take train down the creek and under the C&O main to the yard on the Kanawha River bank, where most of it will be loaded into river barges at a terminal not far up the river from Charleston. (An ex-NKP 2-8-0 is stored in background.) The road went out of business in the late 1980s. but by 2000 was back in business with an industrial switcher as power.

E. L. Huddleston
Kanawha Central no. 1 replaced ex-C&O 2-8-0 no. 944 a year before this photo was taken at Olcott, W.Va. in 1953. The 300 HP diesel, built in 1939 by Plymouth Locomotive Works of Plymouth, Ohio, imitates the looks of a steam locomotive with its sand dome ahead of the cab and an exhaust vent that looks like a smoke stack. (One can trace the front sand pipes from the dome to the wheels.) Two slabs of steel, fore and aft, and embossed "Plymouth," provide ballast to increase the weight on drivers of the small locomotive. Jim Boyd's photo in *American Freight Train* reveals later bright paint job. The KC hauled coal loads down Brier Creek to connection with C&O's line up Big Coal River.

E. L. Huddleston
KC no. 1 starts to work this summer afternoon in 1953. The "engineer's" young son is riding on the fireman's side as the diesel revvs up and heads toward the loading platform east of Olcott, where it wil pick up a coal car or two to take down to the C&O connection at Brounland on C&O's Big Coal Subdivision. Top of cab of former C&O Consolidation no. 944 is visible above engine house door, and its tender, unfortunately, will remain uncoupled until the engine is moved out for scrapping.

Color Pictorial

Summits of the Alleghenies— Getting There

Clinchfield's climb to the "front" of the Cumberland Plateau and the Virginian's and Norfolk and Western's attaining the summit of the Appalachian Plateau involved steep grades. Chesapeake and Ohio, unlike the other three roads, did not have to climb the Appalachian Plateau but did have to climb to the divide between Atlantic and Gulf drainage in the Ridge and Valley Province. Clinchfield crossed the Ridge and Valley Province without much trouble, but N&W and Virginian both climbed "Christiansburg Mountain" between the New and the Great Valley, on the edge of the Ridge and Valley Province.

Everett N. Young

Clinchfield's climb to the Front at Sandy Ridge began at its northern terminus in the Appalachian Plateau at Elkhorn City, Ky. Just south of that junction was a disturbance in the rather even bedding of the sedimentary rocks of the Plateau. Pine Mountain anticline produced cataclysmic displacement of the rock layers along a fault line marking the boundary between Virginia and Kentucky. The passage of the Russell Fork of the Big Sandy through this fault zone produced a gorge and strange rock formations. At the Breaks Interstate Park one can observe this gorge and the railroad through it (now CSX). At Pool Point Tunnel and bridge (out of sight of the tourist) was one of the main construction projects of the CRR's northern extension. High above the river, a southbound coal train in 1977 heads toward Erwin, Tenn.

Everett N. Young

The area of the fault's effect on landscape is called the Breaks of the Big Sandy. At State Line Tunnel, a southbound CSX freight (October 1996) follows the river through the gorge. There being no river "bank" for the right-of-way, the tunnel simply parallels the course of the cliff-lined river.

Clinchfield F7 No. 813 leads two
more units climbing the Blue Ridge
Loops. The complex rock formation
in cut—neither in beds nor folded—shows railroad is in the Blue
Ridge Province.

Second Pigeon Shifter, made famous by
O. Winston Link, is sorting loads by scale
destination on tracks leading to big
Island Creek Coal Co. underground mine
near Delbarton, W.Va. in 1958.

A busy railroad in mighty rough country—that's the two
tunnels at Hemphill, on the Pocahontas Div. Slide detectors
over the tunnel mouth at at left suggest unstable rock layers, probably soft sandstones and shale. Just beyond these
tunnels is Farm, operating point where in steam days tonnage was reduced and pushers added for the climb to the
summit of Great Flattop Mountain. This May 2000 eastbound has a single unit on the head end.

Kurt Reisweber

On the "Poky" Division, pusher engines head west through Coopers toward Farm, where they will probably shove an eastbound to the top of the Plateau at Bluefield. The long tunnel under Great Flattop is not far west of the bridge and tunnel at Coopers. Historic Bluestone Branch (curving across bridge) was gateway to Abbs Valley, where Frederick Kimball and his wife (who gave the name) first viewed the seam Pocahontas no. 3. The sturdy main line bridge was not here before 1950, for it was part of the relocation of the Coaldale summit tunnel.

E.L. Huddleston
Tug Fork is barely visible at right as Class A 1209 accelerates at least 175 loads west on the Scioto Division toward Portsmouth in April, 1957, through Naugatuck, W.Va.

B.D. Martin/TLC Publishing Collection

Class A No. 1211 has its tender heaped with coal as it storms westbound out of Williamson, West Virginia on a beautiful October day, 1957. The mighty Class A was rated at this time for 175 to 190 cars (14,500 tons) of slow freight(or coal) on the mostly level run to Portsmouth, Ohio.

B.D. Martin/TLC Publishing Collection

Williamson was the last outpost of N&W steam power, attracting fans in the last days. Roanoke-built Class S1a switcher No. 205 days are numbered in the October 1957 view at Williamson. He replacements are already surrounding her and she would be retired and sent to scrap just a little over a year later.

E.L. Huddleston

The steam era is not far behind, witness the water column standing mute as four GP9s are taking a mixed freight west under a classic N&W signal bridge on the "Poky" Division west of Iaeger.

Kurt Reisweber

A NS westbound (in 1994) on its way from Roanoke to Bluefield climbs out of the Great Valley to the Ridge and Valley Province toward the summit at Christiansburg. Photographer looks down at cut composed of limestone, which was left when short Shawsville Tunnel was "daylighted" to make possible "double stack" train operation. The tunnel had been a scenic attraction ever since the Virginia and Tennessee RR drilled it in 1853.

For the Virginian (now NS) to climb from the Guyandotte basin at Mullens, West Virginia, to the top of the Appalachian Plateau and then to drop down the Allegheny Front to the New River required grade of 2.07 percent—sufficient reason for electrification. However, two years after this 1960 photo, the "motors" were retired or sold. The three Fairbanks-Morse "Trainmaster" model diesels are for use on coal branch lines surrounding Mullens and the nearby yard at Elmore.

Two 1948 General Electric "motors" on "hot" manifest no. 72 (at left) leave Elmore Yard to climb to the top of the Plateau at Princeton in 1959 and then cross Allegheny Mountain to Roanoke. The class EL-C electric, at right, is newer but not as attractive as the 1948 model.

Kurt Reisweber

In the rift, or "valley" of the East River east of Ingleside, at Oakvale, West Virginia, the former electrified tracks of the Virginian meet the former N&W main line as both sets of tracks descend from the Plateau to the New River before entering the Ridge and Valley Province. The unit coal train originated on the old Virginian at Kopperston and is headed for Hyco, North Carolina.

E.L. Huddleston

The Virginian's Fairbanks-Morse "Trainmaster" diesels had one characteristic, belching great quantities of white or bluish smoke after idling, No. 59 shows this while starting out with a cut of cars at Elmore in this June 1959 scene. This is the east end of Elmore forming a wye, the line to the left is the Guyandotte River line to Gilbert, to the right is the mainline to Princeton. The FM is apparently heading out on the electrified portion to work a mine, while the electrics are returning form shoving an eastbound up the grade.

Kurt Reisweber

The 14 mile climb on the former electrified Virginian from Mullens to the summit involves many bridges and tunnels. In May 1998 NS pushers are returning to Elmore (Mullens) from the summit of Flattop Mountain. Numerous views of this graceful bridge at Covel, West Virginia, have been published but none looking down on it, like this one!

E.L. Huddleston

Along banks of upper Guyandotte an eastbound departs from Elmore yards up the steep grade to top of Appalachian Plateau at Clarks Gap. It takes lots of electrified power to lift the train up 2.07% grade.

Leaving Roanoke, the old Virginian main easily conquered the Blue Ridge by climbing above the level of the Roanoke river by a 0.2% grade until it reached the Piedmont plain that took the line overland to descend Goose Creek. Here at Falling Creek viaduct, an eastbound Norfolk Southern is strung out along the ledge above the river valley. This photo location would have looked even better if someone had pictured a 2-6-6-6 climbing this grade!

Left: On the plateau between the Roanoke River and Goose Creek are several former VGN railroad bridges, including one over Kates Creek just west of Goodview, not far out of Roanoke. An excursion in November 1987, headed by a Southern FP7 diesel, heads from Roanoke to North Carolina. It will leave the old Virginian at Altavista, Va., junction with the Southern.

Below: In October 1990, an NS eastbound enters the passing siding at Huddleston, Va. (named for the Virginian founder's mother) along Goose Creek, which the old Virginian followed eastward in taking a path overland to avoid the deviant course of the Roanoke just east of Roanoke. The creek, subject to frequent flooding, has damaged the right of way, requiring riprap.

Kurt Reisweber

Left: This C&O eastbound coal train, headed for export, has at least 160 loaded coal cars but is powered by just one 3,000H.P. V-16 diesel engine in the "mother" unit, an EMD GP40-2. The second unit, a GP30, was rebuilt to a "slug" at Paducah, Ky., in the late 1980s. That a mother-slug combination can take so much tonnage overland is explained by the fact that the line following the James River from the Alleghenies to Richmond is built on the tow path of an old canal and by the fact that the James cuts a gap through the Blue Ridge about 30 miles farther on near Balcony Falls, Va. This location, at Lyle, is above a tunnel. Across the Great Valley are mountains in the Ridge and Valley Province.

E. L. Huddleston

Below: C&O had two routes across Virginia: one tunnels under the Blue Ridge east of Waynesboro (illustrated here) and the other follows the James River's gap through the Blue Ridge at Balcony Falls. In August 1961, a C&O "special" for Washington exits the tunnel and starts descent of slope of the Blue Ridge at Afton station. The near nine mile descent ends at Crozet, named for the French engineer who built the Blue Ridge around 1855. White building at top is near entrance to Skyline Drive and Blue Ridge Parkway.

Kurt Reisweber

C&O's crossing of the Ridge and Valley Province would have been easier if construction westward had gone up Dunlap Creek, for at the head of this stream, there was easy passage over the Atlantic-Gulf divide to the New River. Instead, the line was located in a higher part of the Alleghenies so it could serve the already established spa at White Sulphur springs, W. Va. In 1985 an eastbound coal train passes empties waiting at Moss Run, Va. One can see how the tracks leave Dunlap Creek Valley (at center) and start through a cleft in the ridge at right so that train can climb to the crest and tunnel under the divide at a spot near White Sulphur. (The cleft is visible to the right of the church at Moss Run.)

> *"The Blue Ridge" --*
> *"Rails across, through,*
> *and beneath the Blue*
> *Ridge amplify the beauty*
> *of this eastern most*
> *mountain range."*

Kurt Reisweber

The Blue Ridge from the Great Smokies in North Carolina to Mt. Rogers in Virginia is a tumbled complex of ridges, and Clinchfield tackles the range from the north by following the fast flowing Nolichucky River, which forms a gorge in its lower reaches before leaving the mountains and entering the Great Valley. A northbound CSX train descends the Nolichucky near Poplar, NC., July 1994.

Riding That New River Train

The New (a better name geologically would be the "Old") is the only river that crosses completely the Ridge and Valley Province and makes a path through the Allegheny Front—the escarpment at the eastern edge of the Appalachian Plateau. Norfolk and Western, Virginian, and Chesapeake and Ohio all made use of the New River in traversing the Appalachian chain. Only the Clinchfield was unable to because the New rises in the Blue Ridge north east of the Clinchfield's main line and flows basically north into south central West Virginia. (Roughly, INT 77 parallels the New.)

Kurt Reisweber

The view from Hawks Nest, both upriver and down (as here) is the most famous along the entire river. Artists came here from Cincinnati in the 1830s to paint the view from the 585 ft. overlook. Lovers Leap, not quite as high as Hawks Nest, is about half a mile up river. A C&O (CSX) westbound is down-grade past the dam that takes the entire flow of the river through Gauley Mountain for electric generation. Around the curve from where the train is now, the tracks will split, one going up the south side and the other crossing and heading up the north side of the New

N&W Photo/K.L. Miller Collection
Both the N&W and Virginian paralleled the New, in a scene from 1950, N&W's famed *Powhatan Arrow* steams west-bound along the New River, the Virginian can be seen on the far side of the river. Here, the New, originating in North Carolina, is cutting across the Great Valley (note low hills beyond). Behind photographer are the New River Palisades and the high ridges of the Ridge and Valley Province.

E. L. Huddleston
Late Saturday afternoon in October 1983, westbound New River excursion pulled by restored Nickel Plate 2-8-4 no. 765 slows to 15 mph at the sharp curve leading to bridge over New River at Hawks Nest station.

E. L. Huddleston
Sewell bridge, some eight miles up the New from Hawks Nest, brings the two main C&O tracks together once again on the north side. Here, in the heart of the Gorge and in worked out coal country an eastbound manifest in 1957 displays car types not seen in service in 2002; namely, a loaded, wooden livestock car, an ice filled wood-sided refrigerator car, and a red caboose.

estbound freight approaches Grandview Overlook.
e Appalachian Plateau, because of a tilt upward (
vel surface evidences plateau surface), produces a
ff top about twice the height of that at Hawks Nest.
poking south (east by railroad direction) one sees piers
middle of the river about 6 miles away that belong to
pandoned bridge for logging road up Glade Creek. At
nton, some 22 miles upriver, C&O (CSX) will leave the
uthward trending New and head up its tributary, the
eenbrier, into the Ridge and Valley Province.

Farther up river from Narrows is a panoramic view of the New
that the photographer worked hard to find. In 1992 an NS train
heads east on old Virginian tracks past connection (newly made
since VGN merger) with N&W's Potts Valley Branch, which was
originally built as the Big Stony Railway. After crossing the New
from N&W connection (at left) the track crossed the old
Virginian and then kept parallel with it until reaching Potts
Creek at Norcross, where the N&W track headed up Potts Creek
Valley (out of sight around the bend). Long ridges in back are
East River Mountain and Peters Mountain.

Surrounded by lofty parallel ridges of the Ridge and Valley Province the New River has cut a course into a limestone upland leaving beautiful cliffs on both sides of the river roughly from Pembroke to Eggleston. The cliffs at Eggleston were named Ballard Rock after the first climber, and at one time a mineral springs resort was here. Company photographer (and power director at the Narrows power house) had EL-2B No. 126 posed with an eastbound coal train at the Palisades long enough to shoot 8 transparencies, one of which was used on the cover of Virginian's last annual report for the year 1958. This image is digitally restored from the faded original Ektachrome transparency.

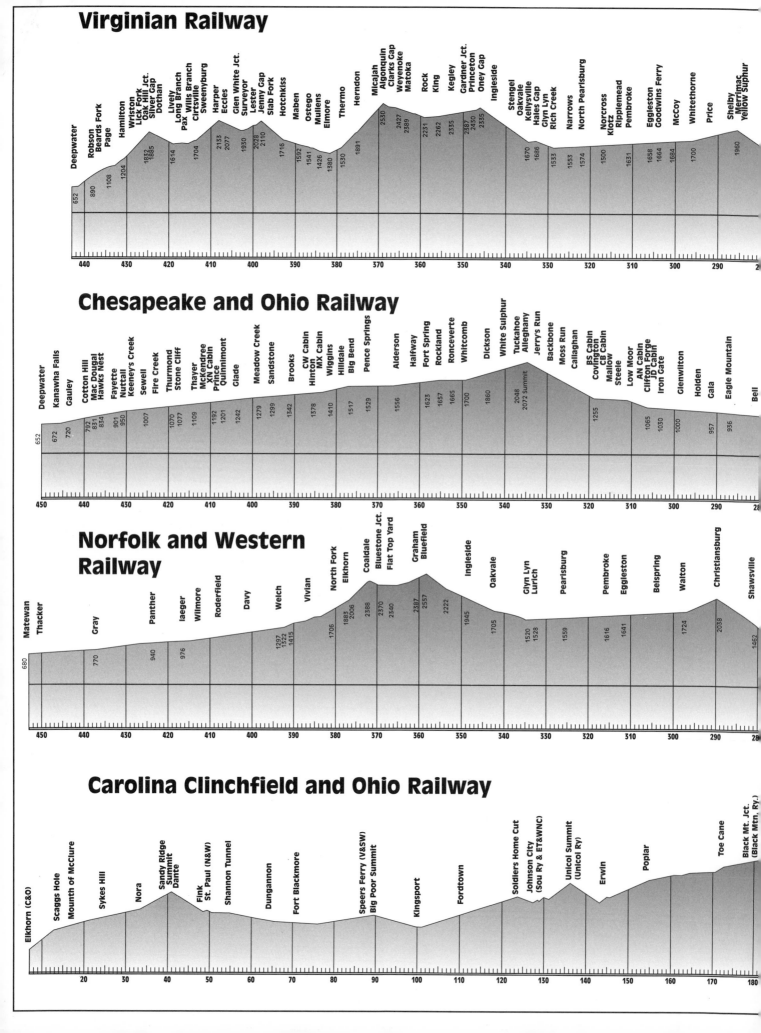

Virginian Railway

Deepwater 652 · Robson 890 · Beards Fork · Page 1108 · Hamilton 1204 · Wriston · Lick Fork · Oak Hill Jct. 1852 · Silver Gap 1885 · Dothan · Lively 1614 · Long Branch · Pax · Wills Branch 1704 · Cirtsville · Sweenyburg · Harper 2153 · Eccles 2077 · Glen White Jct. · Surveyor 1930 · Lester · Jenny Gap 2028 · Slab Fork 2110 · Hotchkiss 1716 · Maben 1592 · Ostego 1541 · Mullens 1426 · Elmore 1380 · Thermo 1530 · Herndon 1891 · Micajah 2530 · Algonquin · Clarks Gap 2427 · Weyenoke 2389 · Matoka · Rock 2251 · King 2262 · Kegley 2335 · Gardner Jct. 2387 · Princeton 2450 · Oney Gap 2335 · Ingleside · Stengel · Oakvale 1670 · Kellysville 1686 · Hales Gap · Glyn Lyn 1533 · Rich Creek · Narrows 1553 · North Pearisburg 1574 · Norcross 1500 · Klotz · Ripplemead · Pembroke 1631 · Eggleston 1658 · Goodwins Ferry 1664 · McCoy 1684 · Whitethorne · Price 1700 · Shelby · Merrimac 1960 · Yellow Sulphur

440 · 430 · 420 · 410 · 400 · 390 · 380 · 370 · 360 · 350 · 340 · 330 · 320 · 310 · 300 · 290

Chesapeake and Ohio Railway

Deepwater 652 · Kanawha Falls 672 · Gauley 720 · Cotton Hill 792 · Mac Dougal 831 · Hawks Nest 834 · Fayette 901 · Nuttall 950 · Keeney's Creek 1007 · Sewell · Fire Creek · Thurmond 1070 · Stone Cliff 1077 · Thayer 1109 · McKendree · XN Cabin 1192 · Prince 1201 · Quinnimont 1242 · Glade · Meadow Creek 1279 · Sandstone 1299 · Brooks 1342 · CW Cabin · Hinton 1378 · MX Cabin · Wiggins 1410 · Hilldale · Big Bend 1517 · Pence Springs 1529 · Alderson 1556 · Halfway · Fort Spring 1623 · Rockland 1657 · Ronceverte 1665 · Whitcomb 1700 · Dickson 1860 · White Sulphur · Tuckahoe 2048 · Alleghany 2072 Summit · Jerry's Run · Backbone · Moss Run · Callaghan 1255 · BS Cabin · Covington · CB Cabin · Mallow · Steele · Low Moor 1065 · AN Cabin · Clifton Forge 1030 · JD Cabin · Iron Gate 1000 · Glenwilton · Holden 957 · Gala 936 · Eagle Mountain · Bell

450 · 440 · 430 · 420 · 410 · 400 · 390 · 380 · 370 · 360 · 350 · 340 · 330 · 320 · 310 · 300 · 290 · 280

Norfolk and Western Railway

Matewan · Thacker 680 · Gray 770 · Panther 940 · Iaeger 976 · Wilmore · Roderfield · Davy 1297 · Welch 1322 · Vivian 1415 · North Fork 1706 · Elkhorn 1883 · Coaldale 2006 · Bluestone Jct. 2388 · Flat Top Yard 2370 · 2340 · Graham 2387 · Bluefield 2557 · 2222 · Ingleside 1945 · Oakvale 1705 · Glyn Lyn 1520 · Lurich 1528 · Pearisburg 1559 · Pembroke 1616 · Eggleston 1641 · Belspring 1724 · Walton · Christiansburg 2038 · Shawsville 1462

450 · 440 · 430 · 420 · 410 · 400 · 390 · 380 · 370 · 360 · 350 · 340 · 330 · 320 · 310 · 300 · 290 · 280

Carolina Clinchfield and Ohio Railway

Elkhorn (C&O) · Scaggs Hole · Mounth of McClure · Sykes Hill · Nora · Sandy Ridge Summit · Dante · Fink · St. Paul (N&W) · Shannon Tunnel · Dungannon · Fort Blackmore · Speers Ferry (V&SW) · Big Poor Summit · Kingsport · Fordtown · Soldiers Home Cut · Johnson City (Sou Ry & ET&WNC) · Unicol Summit (Unicol Ry) · Erwin · Poplar · Toe Cane · Black Mt. Jct. (Black Mtn. Ry.)

20 · 30 · 40 · 50 · 60 · 70 · 80 · 90 · 100 · 110 · 120 · 130 · 140 · 150 · 160 · 170 · 180